Liberal Evangelism

Liberal Evangelism

JOHN SAXBEE

First published in Great Britain 1994
Society for Promoting Christian Knowledge
Holy Trinity Church
Marylebone Road
London NW1 4DU

British Library Cataloguing-in-Publication Data

A catalogue record for this book is available from the
British Library

ISBN 0-281-04691-3

Typeset by Pioneer Associates, Perthshire
Printed in Great Britain by
Biddles Ltd, Guildford and King's Lynn

For Jackie

Contents

Preface

This book contains some theory, some theology—and a good deal of practical application. Because responsiveness to practical situations and circumstances is a key theme, it might have been appropriate to start there, and then move on to the theory and theological reflection. However, the sheer enormity of the perceived gap between liberalism and evangelism required a prior account of how that gap could be bridged. Consequently, chapters 1 and 2 have a more academic 'feel' than chapters 3 and 4. So those who prefer practice to theory can start the book half-way through and still get the gist of it all! Having said that, it is to be hoped that most readers will want to engage with the theological scene-setting that seeks to explain the gap as well as trying to bridge it.

John Saxbee
November 1993

1

Liberalism and Evangelism

The persistence of liberalism

In a large department store, you can choose whether to use the stairs or take the lift when making your way from floor to floor. Climbing the stairs will demand effort, and it will involve you being exposed to both the temptations and the delights of each successive department. Taking the lift is easier; as you occupy your secure little room, you move through the various floors safe from direct involvement with any department with which you do not care to do business. The user of the lift, like many religious conservatives, inhabits a secure and unchanging environment, while on the stairs we see the theological liberals struggling to come to terms with each new department and having to decide how to spend what he or she has available and how to choose wisely from what is on offer. As we near the end of the twentieth century, more and more people are being encouraged to take the safe and secure 'lift' of Christian conservatism—with the operators not so much telling the lift occupant what is available floor by floor, as telling the floor staff what is available in the lift! Thus Christianity passes uncontaminated through the core of successive cultures like the air-conditioned lift through the shaft of a departmental store. But what if the stairs provide the only means whereby Christianity can truly develop its identity by engaging creatively—and, therefore, evangelistically—with a variety of historical, geographical and social institutions? It may be laborious, risky, full of potential distractions—but if Jesus ever took the lift, it was from the mountain top after his resurrection; before that, it was all done the hard way!

Now, picture language of this kind is bound to put *everyone's* nose out of joint! The liberals will resent the implication that they are indecisive, manipulable and subject to the blandishments of every passing fashion. Conservatives will take strong exception to their depiction as security-conscious separatists—and lazy to boot! And no one will like the all-too-flippant attempt to recruit none other than our Lord himself to support this tasteless caricature. These objections aside, the picture may just have got us into the way of thinking about how one group of Christians relate to the practice of evangelism in a decade when their conservative counterparts have dictated, and been allowed to dictate, much of the agenda. It is these representatives of liberal Christianity who will take centre stage in this study, and we shall begin by setting out our reasons for attempting to define and promote a liberal approach to evangelism.[1]

The tendency to write off theological liberalism has surfaced with almost monotonous regularity throughout this century. Barr suggests that fundamentalists see 'liberalism' and 'modernism' as 'no more than necessary myths—bogeys that have to be held up for execration and ritual contempt on every possible occasion'.[2] Of course it depends on what you mean by 'liberalism', and we will need to try to spell out what is meant by the word in this context; however, it is still likely that any use of the term will induce a negative knee-jerk response in some quarters. Indeed, there are two statements about liberal Christianity that would probably command general assent among a broad range of contemporary commentators: (i) it had its day, and (ii) it's had its day. The former statement might well be accompanied by a sense of sympathy or even sneaking admiration, but not much regret. The latter statement is likely to be accompanied either by a sense of nostalgia or triumphalist relief. Somewhat paternalistically, liberals are depicted as well-meaning, sympathetic figures, who have their hearts in the right place, but are ultimately misguided and pathologically gullible with regard to the claims of the modern world. Opponents of liberalism argue that events of the twentieth century have shown liberalism up for the lightweight, short-sighted pipedream that it really is—and it's had its day!

In the face of this corporate onslaught, there has been a tendency for liberals to abdicate their ground and veer off to the left or right, or simply to curl up and die. A siege mentality undermines self-confidence, such that the liberal position becomes increasingly difficult to sustain against overwhelming odds. Yet the liberal tendency refuses to go away. Still there persists within mainstream Christianity a significant body of believers whose approach to Christian believing, belonging and behaving is essentially liberal in style and substance. It is in the nature of the case that they will not be conspicuously self-assertive in the promotion of their point of view, so their numerical strength can be easily underestimated. However, periodic *causes célèbres*—usually involving controversial utterances by prelates in high places—trigger debates that are notable for the quantity and quality of what can only be described as liberal argument. As long ago as 1939, Robert Calhoun of Yale wrote an autobiographical article entitled 'A Liberal Bandaged but Unbowed'[3] and, more recently, the Archbishop of York has written his *Confessions of a Conservative Liberal.*[4] These titles convey something of the defensive and apologetic tone of much liberal theology this century, but they also represent the persistence of the liberal tendency against considerable odds. It is this persistence that we seek to honour and affirm, especially in a decade when an emphasis on evangelism might add to the liberal's sense of insecurity and marginalization.

Furthermore, the extent of liberal belief must not be limited to the ranks of the professional theologians. It is indeed essential that liberal theology 'gets out of hard covers'[5] and breaks free from any sense that it is a dilettante diversion for sceptical intellectuals. It could well be that those of a liberal persuasion comprise the silent majority in the congregations of the mainstream Churches, and those involved in adult education programmes testify to the prevalence of liberal thinking across a wide range of participants. There may be those who would wish to isolate liberalism within an intellectual ghetto in order to dilute its incidence and influence, but that is not how it feels to those who are in close touch with a broad cross-section of church membership in Britain and the United States. Of course, statistics are notoriously difficult to evaluate when it comes to calibrating religious convictions,[6] and so it will be for the reader to reflect on just how many people of their acquaintance subscribe to the tendency described as 'liberal' in these pages.

Some will be numbered among the 'creatively disaffiliated' who are trying to pursue an honest religious quest outside the structures of institutionalized religion. More often than not, they will be faithful, thoughtful folk with a determined Christian commitment that they may find difficult to articulate in what they sometimes experience as the hostile climate of conservative triumphalism on the one hand and rootless relativism on the other. Again, it has to be said that this climate can feel all the more hostile when evangelism is the key issue of the hour and commitment to evangelism becomes the litmus test for genuine Christian allegiance.

The challenge of evangelism

At the back of all this is the assumption that liberalism is antithetical to evangelism, and that those committed to evangelism are unlikely to be of a liberal disposition. To an extent, this assumption is based on fundamental misunderstandings of what liberal Christianity actually stands for. However, responsibility must also be laid at the door of liberalism itself, in so far as it has sought to define itself and its mission in ways that explicitly distance it from the evangelistic task. If it is true that liberal Christianity has been so busy transforming the faith that it has forgotten to transmit it, then liberals only have themselves to blame if they are ruled off-side when a Decade of Evangelism is initiated.

Memories of the 1960s live long in the minds of those who lived through that extraordinary decade when the torch was deemed to have passed to a new generation with respect to politics, society, morality and theology. David Bosch has observed how, at the time of the WCCF Uppsala General Assembly in 1968, 'it was hard to define exactly how mission differed from the ethos and activities of the Peace Corps'.[7] Many liberals are still struggling to get a grip on evangelism in the modern world and some of the impetus for this book derives from an encounter with members of the Peace Corps in Rwanda in 1988. My reason for visiting that small, beautiful, densely populated and pathetically poor East African country was to represent the General Synod of the Church of England at a Partners in Mission Consultation called by the Francophone Provinces of Rwanda,

Burundi and Zaire. The evangelical Ruanda Mission clearly had the strongest influence on the African Church there, with conservative theology and evangelistic zeal combining to dramatic effect as part of the great East African Revival. There was much here to celebrate and admire, even as one tried to face the awesome realities of political oppression, grinding poverty and the pernicious AIDS epidemic. During my stay it became increasingly more difficult for me to feel content with the pressures and processes of the prevailing evangelistic strategy when the context demanded revolutionary changes in the ordering of economic and political priorities, especially on the part of the erstwhile colonial powers in that part of Africa. My change in perspective was partly brought about when four volunteers with the US Peace Corps moved into rooms next to mine in the Diocesan Guest House in Kigali, the Rwandan capital. All my liberal instincts attracted me to their cause as they set aside two precious years from their promising careers in the United States to come to Africa, learn the relevant languages, and work alongside local people as ambassadors of social and humanitarian development.

Fortunately, when it comes to evaluating the virtues of evangelistic and developmental programmes, it is not a question of 'either/or', but in my own mind there was little doubt that I would line up alongside the Peace Corps Volunteers if such a choice became necessary. Yet they had no common religious convictions, and their motivation was unashamedly humanistic. If my sympathies and sentiments lay with them more than with the evangelical missionary society, then to what extent did I, as a liberal in poverty-stricken Africa, have a gospel to proclaim that was in any way distinguishable from the secularized assumptions of the Peace Corps? My reading in modern mission strategies had kept me well-informed with regard to the oft-repeated skirmishes between the so-called 'fundamentalists' on the one hand, and supposed adherents of 'the social gospel' on the other. Now, though, this battle was being fought out in my own experience as I sought to make a positive contribution to the cause of mission in Africa—without simply indulging in the luxury of theological fiddling while the fires of impoverishment and overpopulation threatened to overwhelm my new-found brothers and sisters in Christ. Time was simply too short to perpetuate that dialogue of the deaf that has characterized much of what has passed for debate between liberals and evangelicals with respect to the content and style of Christian evangelism. It is necessary to rethink liberalism in such a way as to demonstrate its essentially evangelistic purpose, and to rethink evangelism in such a way as to ensure the contribution of liberal insights to a balanced and coherent strategy for living and sharing the good news of God in this and every decade. In short, a liberal approach to evangelism is called for, and what follows is offered as a contribution to that end.

However, this project does not owe its origins exclusively to the challenge posed by personal experience of the Church overseas. That experience simply served to focus issues that had been indistinctly present in a busy parochial and educational ministry over a period of twenty years. As a theological liberal I had not found it too difficult to express my theology through preaching, teaching, liturgy, counselling and pastoral care. However, it was far less clear to me how evangelism fitted into my ministerial agenda—apart from taking the viewpoint 'it's all evangelism in the end, though, isn't it?' And so it is, but deep down I knew that this kind of riposte in the face of challenges from evangelical colleagues was far from satisfactory and seriously short on theological substance. Yet it was clearly the case that many who would resist being described as 'evangelists' for fear of the company they might be assumed to be keeping, were still winning people for the gospel through the day-to-day exercise of their Christian witness. If they were not in fact engaging in 'evangelism', then the word is obviously in need of some redefinition.

Likewise, if a theology, including liberal theology, does not entail a consequential evangelistic strategy, then there are good grounds for arguing that this is not Christian theology at all. The 'post-liberal' theologian Hans Frei argues that theology must stick to being purely descriptive with respect to the internal logic of biblical faith, and thus 'not to worry overmuch about how non-believers become believers'. In contrast, Bosch asserts that contemporary New Testament scholars are now affirming what the systematic theologian Martin Kahler said in the early years of this century: that mission is 'the Mother of Theology'.[8] Kahler goes on to assert that Christian theology began as 'an accompanying manifestation of the Christian mission' and not as 'a luxury in a world-dominating church'. The New Testament writers wrote in the context of an 'emergency situation', of a Church that, because of its missionary encounter with the world, was *forced* to theologize. So theology and missiology are inextricably linked and, because evangelism is a necessary aspect in mission and not merely a contingent facet, theology and evangelism are mutually entailed. To espouse liberalism without clarity concerning a liberal approach to evangelism is tantamount to denying that one's theology is truly Christian in any New Testament or subsequent meaning of the word.

We shall attempt to describe the approach to evangelism implicit in liberal theology, and we shall also seek to show how any evangelistic initiative that does not make room for such a liberal approach alongside others in its range of strategic possibilities will be seriously deficient. Evangelism needs to be liberal, just as liberalism needs to be evangelistic—a bold claim in view of the wedge that has been driven between them over the course of this century. It is surely the case that the Decade of Evangelism will be seriously impoverished without the contribution of a liberal approach, and liberalism will deserve to be marginalized if it cannot nurture and sustain an effective evangelistic contribution within contemporary culture.

Indeed, some of the energy for the enterprise arises from frustration, and not a little indignation, with respect to what passes for evangelism as this Decade unfolds. There is a need to 'decode' the Decade in order to see more clearly just what are the assumptions at work here—and to offer a critique that will be both positive and creative in the face of the evangelistic challenge. For now, let it be said that a degree of triumphalism and paternalism has been apparent in some of the Decade literature, sufficient to cause genuine concern among those of a liberal persuasion. Some predicted that this would be the case and have simply washed their hands of the whole business, giving it up as a bad job. Others want to affirm the Decade in principle, while regretting that the widest range of theological and personal resources are not being brought to bear on the task. It is in the latter spirit that we offer this liberal approach to evangelism. While we might well entertain serious reservations concerning the methods and content of certain evangelistic enterprises, we will still want to see our proposals as making a contribution alongside, rather than in competition with, alternative styles and strategies.

However, if it is the case that 'the central intellectual motive of liberal theology is to make the Christian faith *intelligible* and *credible*, comprehensive *and* convincing to intelligent, informed and honest minds of each successive era',[9] then liberals must challenge approaches to evangelism that tend to encourage intellectual dishonesty and naive credulity.[10] On the other hand, the motive behind liberal theology must be more than merely 'intellectual', so that the need remains for liberals to discern and promote ways of sharing the Christian faith that respond to every dimension of human experience—physical, emotional, experiential as well as intellectual—and to be positively challenged by those approaches to evangelism that tend to get beyond the intellect to those parts that liberalism has so often failed to reach. While there are good grounds for sharing Hugh Dawes's vision of a liberal or 'open' Christianity freed from an 'obsessive concern for recruitment' (his rather tendentious synonym for evangelism),[11] it cannot be denied that, as a liberal Christian, my desire is to swell the ranks of liberal Christians and to do so not only from among those who are currently of an alternative Christian persuasion, but also from among those who do not call themselves Christian at all. What is that if it is not a commitment to evangelism?

Bridging the gulf

This brings me to the most powerful motive of all impelling this project. Henry van Dusen posed the question, 'Where is the locus of Christian truth and authority?', and answered as follows:

> Liberal Theology locates the decisive norm at one place: the mind and especially the faith of Jesus. . . . Liberal Theology in each of its authentic expressions has been through and through Christocentric, indeed, it has been the most determinedly and consistently Christocentric Theology in Christian history.[12]

More recently, writing from a decisively liberal perspective, John Bowden has described Jesus as 'a clue to how the world is, to how we are, and how God is',[13] and Hugh Dawes endorses 'that fundamental christian perception . . . that God was seen and known in a human life in Jesus'.[14] To identify Jesus, and to identify oneself with Jesus and to help others to identify themselves with him, are essential ingredients of Christian evangelism—because, as 'the very embodiment of God's power and reality', Jesus puts people in touch with God.[15] How this is so is the fundamental issue for all evangelistic strategies, but above all for a liberal approach to evangelism that builds on such an essentially Christocentric liberal theology. If indeed God is as God is in Jesus, then any Christian whose life is centred on such a God must be restless so long as lives are centred elsewhere. Such restlessness may be calmed by the conviction that such lives are in touch with God other than through Jesus, and openness to such a possibility is a defining characteristic of liberalism. Yet it is conviction with respect to the genuine God-centredness of those lives that is crucial and, for Christians, it is Jesus who offers criteria by means of which to evaluate what is, and is not, of God.

In a pluralist environment, Christians have to face questions like 'Why choose Christianity rather than other possibilities for life?' and to be able to answer positively 'without making claims to uniqueness and ultimacy that have become hard to sustain in mixed company'.[16] Liberals are not alone in facing this challenge, and it is tempting to adopt Dawes's moratorium on 'recruitment' so as to avoid the risk of causing offence in such 'mixed company'. However, this cannot be right when we know that there are lives governed by values, meanings and purposes that are unworthy of God as realized in Jesus. To work for the choosing of Christianity in such circumstances must be a legitimate object for liberal Christians, and an appropriate approach to such a task is the main burden of this book. Liberals can readily affirm and celebrate lives that, on the face of it, owe nothing to the influence of Jesus or his followers but that more than meet the evaluative criteria of a Christocentric theology. Liberals, though, cannot sit by and settle for anything less for themselves or for others, hence the evangelistic imperative to put people in touch with God is as crucial for them as for anyone else.

We are set to argue for the bridging of the gap between liberalism and evangelism that has been allowed to grow to such an extent that it is widely believed to be essentially unbridgeable.

Bridge-building involves commitment to the enterprise on both sides of the divide, and that is why it is necessary to acknowledge that evangelism has greater breadth, and liberalism greater depth, than is sometimes allowed. Hugh Dawes is justified in his charge that 'there is a lot of name-calling going on within mainstream christianity at present . . . and liberalism has been singled out as its target',[17] but he then goes in for a prodigious amount of name-calling himself against 'conservatives' and 'traditionalists'. However, if we are going to arrive at what David Bosch calls a 'relevant missiology' for the twenty-first century, then it must be marked by a readiness to enter into a situation of creative tension with respect to views other than our own. Flexibility must be the controlling factor as Christianity continues its age-old struggle to engage with the claims and counter-claims of consecutive cultures.

For example, we can take a moment to examine how the Enlightenment has been all too readily adopted as the whipping-boy with respect to the ills of modern Western culture. Show up the Enlightenment for what it is, so the argument runs, and it will be clearly seen that Christian collusion with Enlightenment assumptions must now give way to the reinstatement of revealed religion as the controlling judge of truth and error. Nevertheless, it is something of a tribute to the influence and penetration of Enlightenment perspectives that they continue to command so much attention some two hundred years after Kant and Hume added their philosophical weight to that revolution in human thought and self-perception that can be traced back to the advent of printing, the creative flowering of the Renaissance, and the scientific innovations of Galileo and Newton.

Briefly, the Enlightenment was 'a declaration of independence by the human subject, from every limitation but faithfulness to him/herself'[18] and it is this 'turn to the subject' that captures the essence of the paradigm shift from medieval and Reformation reliance on external and revealed authority. This led to a consequential emphasis on freedom, and 'the insatiable appetite for freedom to live as one pleases, developed into a virtually inviolable right in the Western "democratism".[19] The subjectiveness of the Enlightenment also called into question notions of objective reality so that 'culturally decisive was the policy of persistence in the critique of appearances'.[20] This opened up whole new adventures in scientific inquiry with all that followed—for better and, reluctant though they were to admit it, for worse. This in its turn led to a mechanistic world-view, with the consequent elimination of theological explanations for how and why things are as they are. Knowledge of the laws of cause and effect would enable human beings to master the material world and so progress inexorably towards a state of perfection. The frenetic accumulation and dissemination of facts via the faculties of reason and experience ensured a consequential downgrading of values to the status of mere opinions, with religious beliefs reduced to little more than scurrilous substitutes for rigorous thought.[21] Above all, the Enlightenment was a crusade against claims to Absolute Truth that theologians or metaphysical philosophers might seek to impose as a constraint on the freedom of individuals to pursue truth wherever it might lead.

As Keith Ward has shown, this conviction that the truth must be pursued at all costs was itself a value judgement rather than a truth of physics[22]—metaphysical rather than physical—so that the door was left ajar for the reinstatement of values. It has been pushed open even further, though, by the effective demolition of reductionist philosophies such as positivism and materialism and the emergence of a probabilistic scientific world-view that seems to owe more to neo-orthodoxy than to Newton!

However, the fact of the matter is that these developments in the formation of Western thought presented a comprehensive and ultimately irresistible challenge to the truth-claims of Christianity in so far as these related to what there is to be known about the world and how we come to know it. The consequential Enlightenment culture no longer felt itself totally dependent upon religion for its access to reality—temporal reality, anyway. This means that religious people had to choose between denying the claims of modern knowledge, adapt religious claims to accommodate such knowledge, or enter into creative engagement with modernity so as to affirm the Christian way in the light of, and not in spite of, the Enlightenment. The middle course, that of adaptation, was quickly shown to be unacceptable to the integrity of either religion or science. The other two options became associated with conservatives or fundamentalists on the one hand and liberals and modernists on the other. The liberal approach has commanded a broad-based support over the last two centuries, and even when it has been felt necessary to challenge certain unacceptable cultural trends or assumptions, it has been consistently acknowledged that Christianity since the Enlightenment has needed to interact creatively with modern culture rather than enter into separation. The conservative option, though, has never been abandoned, with the various revivals of the eighteenth and nineteenth centuries fuelling the demands for modern culture to admit the charge of *lèse-majesté* and submit once again to the bar of revelation with respect to truths that will be good for both time and eternity. It is now widely acknowledged that an anti-Enlightenment mood is in the ascendancy in Europe and North America, and that churches that promote such a mood are growing so fast that they themselves have become the 'mainstream' churches in place of mainline Liberal Protestant denominations.[23]

The trouble is that there has been a failure to acknowledge that even if Enlightenment ideas are found wanting, and they are by no means immune from criticism, the whole Enlightenment phenomenon has clearly shown the claims of culture to be distinct from those of religion, so that the relationship between religion and culture remains a challenging issue not only for the age of Enlightenment—but for pre- and post-Enlightenment cultures as well. Before the Enlightenment, it was possible to see Christendom as a seamless robe embracing all facets of life, be they what we would now call secular or sacred. This view did less than justice to the actual cultural situation of early Christianity and it is significant that it is the new historical consciousness associated with the Enlightenment that has helped us to see how the Christian Church acquired its identity by interaction with the prevailing culture before it became the prevailing culture itself. This awareness of cultural relativity has been the single most important contribution made by the Enlightenment to our understanding of how Christianity is to be believed and shared in successive generations. We cannot dis-invent the Enlightenment in order to re-invent Christendom. Christendom assumed that Christianity and culture were coterminous and coincidental, but the reality is that Christianity has to find itself and be found in specific cultural contexts as it engages with and responds to those cultures of which it is itself a part. To be liberal means to take this reality seriously, and that is why liberalism is essentially a child of the Enlightenment—not because it feels obliged to endorse every idea and utterance of the parent, but because it was the Enlightenment that told the truth about Christianity and culture, even if it sometimes failed to tell the truth about other things. To treat the Enlightenment as a catch-all for the ills of modern life with a view to exorcizing its influence prior to the reinstatement of pre-modern structures of knowledge and belief is not only impossible, but fundamentally dishonest. Bridge-building between conservatism and liberalism will involve the honest acknowledgement on the one hand that the Enlightenment got it right with respect to the influence of culture on traditional truth claims and, on the other, that the Enlightenment erred alarmingly with respect to, for example, its belief in progress and its unsustainable optimism regarding human nature.[24]

Thus this book is about liberalism—but especially about a liberal approach to evangelism. It is about the significance of culture for our understanding of the Christian gospel and the extent to which evangelism may be as much about the listening ear as the persuasive tongue, as much about responding as pronouncing. Because liberalism seeks to commend a positive relationship between Christianity and culture, and so avoids any tendency to deny or decry cultural influences on the development of belief and practice, so we shall seek to celebrate pluralism and change as encouragements to openness and flexibility in our approach to evangelism.

The main burden of the case will be set out in chapters 3 and 4, where it will become clear that what is being commended here is not new. My contention is that this kind of approach to evangelism is already being adopted by countless people who may or may not describe themselves as liberals or their activities as evangelistic. At a time when it is easy to feel pressurized into a sense of guilt about being liberal or not being committed to evangelism, it may help if some people recognize themselves in these pages, and are thereby able to see their role and contribution within a missionary agenda that they might otherwise have found difficult to recognize as their own.

First of all, though, we will need to give some account of liberalism and evangelism in the light of such understandings—and misunderstandings—as are current in the contemporary Church.

Notes

1. In spite of the fact that it would probably have been better all round if the word 'evangelization' had been used uniformly across the denominational spectrum, we recognize that the term 'evangelism' has had greater currency in Anglican and Reformed Churches, and we will use it here.
2. J. Barr, *Fundamentalism*. SCM Press 1977, p. 104.
3. Robert Calhoun, 'A Liberal Bandaged but Unbowed', *The Christian Century*, May 1939.
4. J. Habgood, *Confessions of a Conservative Liberal*. SPCK 1988.
5. Haddon Willmer, *Crucible*, January–March 1992, p. 38.
6. See, for example, William McKinney and Wade Clark Roof, 'Liberal Protestantism: A Sociodemographic Perspective', in Robert S. Michaelsen and Wade Clark Roof, *Liberal Protestantism*. New York, Pilgrim Press, 1986.
7. David J. Bosch, *Transforming Mission*. New York, Orbis, 1991, pp. 326–7.
8. M. Kahler, *Schriften zur Christologie und Mission*. Translated and quoted by Bosch in *Transforming Mission*, p. 16.
9. H. P. van Dusen, *The Vindication of Liberal Theology*. New York, Scribner's, 1963, p. 27.
10. Indeed, William Abraham's *The Logic of Evangelism* (Hodder & Stoughton 1989 p. v.) is commended on the basis of C. S. Lewis's plea for evangelists of the head as well as evangelists of the heart.
11. Hugh Dawes, *Freeing the Faith*. SPCK 1992, p. 98.
12. van Dusen, *The Vindication of Liberal Theology*, p. 93. See also C. Marsh, *Questioning Evangelism*, Grove Books 1993, pp. 9–10: 'Liberalism is unreservedly "Christocentric".'
13. J. Bowden, *Jesus: The Unanswered Questions*. SCM 1988, p. 207.
14. Dawes, *Freeing the Faith*, p. 31.
15. David E. Jenkins, *Still Living with Questions*. SCM Press 1990, p. 33.
16. Haddon Willmer, 'Taking Responsibility', in *20/20 Visions*. SPCK 1992, p. 151.
17. Dawes, *Freeing the Faith*, p. 1.
18. Robert W. Jenson, in David F. Ford, ed., *The Modern Theologians*, vol. 1. Basil Blackwell 1989, p. 26.
19. Bosch, *Transforming Mission*, p. 267.
20. Jenson; see note 18.
21. See L. Newbigin, *Foolishness to the Greeks—The Gospel and Western Culture*. SPCK 1986, chapter 1.
22. Keith Ward, *A Vision to Pursue*. SCM Press 1991, p. 140.
23. See Benton Johnson, 'Liberal Protestantism: The End of the Road', *Annals of the American Academy of Political and Social Science*, July 1985, pp. 39–52.
24. See Bosch, *Transforming Mission*, pp. 351–62.

2

The Liberal Tendency

Charlie Ives could hear two tunes at once. He inherited this ability from his father George who, as the band-master in the small town of Danbury, Connecticut, would arrange for his own band and another one to march past each other in Main Street while each played a different piece. It seems that the local population were not sympathetic to George's experiments, which they heard simply as a discordant cacophony. However, his young son heard something that greatly influenced his own creativity as he developed into one of America's greatest composers.[1] Charles Ives is now honoured for his innovative music, which pre-empted European atonal music by several decades, and among his most celebrated compositions are those that recapture experiences in the Danbury of his childhood by the weaving together of simultaneous melodies, harmonies and rhythms. People at the time thought he 'had his ears on wrong',[2] and it was not until some years after his death in 1954 that an audience began to emerge for these daring, sometimes bewildering, but always compelling, compositions.

During the nineteenth century it became increasingly necessary for Christian believers to come to terms with hearing two tunes at once. While one band marched up the street to the traditional strains of revealed religion, from the opposite direction came a band of miscellaneous moderns improvising for all they were worth on the instruments of science and reason. So long as they were at some distance from each other, it was possible to contemplate the scenario with amused detachment, but a state of confusion was bound to prevail at the point of meeting. Some tried to hang on to one tune and shut out the other, others tried to harmonize the two, while yet others simply covered their ears until peace had been restored! There were those, though, who became excited by the ways in which this encounter opened up new possibilities for sensing and making sense of God, the world and human experience. Like Charles Ives, they tried to hear both tunes at once and could thereby enter a world of sense and meaning that transcended what either could achieve on its own. It is this tendency to want to hear two tunes at once that characterizes liberal Christianity as it seeks to live creatively with the truth-claims of both traditional orthodoxy and post-Enlightenment modernism. It is the attempt to listen to Christendom and contemporary culture simultaneously and to hear, even through the apparent discords, the truths of eternity in tune with today.

We have already used the word 'tendency' to describe Christian liberalism, and it is important to recognize that it is indeed what Galloway termed 'a style of doing theology rather than a school of thought'.[3] Even so, Allan Galloway is referring here to what he calls '*the* liberal theology' (my emphasis) that 'dominated the end of the nineteenth and the beginning of the twentieth century up to about 1920'. While the liberal spirit pervades theological thinking for some decades either side of that period, it is to such figures as Albrecht Ritschl (1822–89), Wilhelm Herrmann (1846–1922), Adolf Harnack (1851–1930), Jean Réville (1854–1907), Ralph Waldo Emerson (1803–82), Horace Bushnell (1802–76) and Henry Scott Holland (1847–1918) that we look for what came closest to becoming a liberal 'school of thought'. However, what unites even these stars in the liberal firmament is more a matter of style than substance. It was the tendency to want to hear both tunes that unified these otherwise highly individualist contributors into what has come to be known as Liberal Protestantism.

In addition, Jean Réville maintained that 'A moderately orthodox believer may practise liberalism; he will not thereby become a Liberal Protestant',[4] along with the implication that liberals are to be found outside the confines of the Liberal Protestant 'school of thought'. The matter is further complicated by the fact that those who belonged to the theological school of Liberal Protestantism may not have recognized themselves as natural members of those Churches (especially in the United States) that are conventionally described as Liberal Protestant. These institutionalized forms of liberal Christianity are best described and evaluated in sociological terms,[5] while Liberal Protestantism as a theological movement 'can best be determined by a study of its historical emergence and progress'.[6] However, we will still want to be clear about the essential characteristics of the liberal tendency at a time when, as John Habgood has put it, 'the word "liberal" . . . has become positively chameleon-like'.[7]

Now the conventional wisdom is that the only thing definite about liberal Christianity is its lack of definition! Most articles and books on the subject will begin with a disclaimer to that effect, and it is for this reason that the liberal label has become synonymous with woolly thinking and wishy-washy morality. The average liberal is assumed to be politically pink, theologically grey, and morally indistinguishable from the prevailing landscape! So let us be clear what is meant by the word 'liberal' in the context of a liberal approach to evangelism, for we believe that there is something very definite and distinctive here that mainstream Christianity can ill afford to neglect.

The marks of a liberal

In his 'Vindication of Liberal Theology', Henry van Dusen describes how, at its birth, it was

> the child of two parents, as every proper child should be: on the one hand, the *intellectual outlook* of the late nineteenth and early twentieth centuries, the Age in which it arose; on the other hand, the *religious resurgence* of that same period.[8]

It will be noticed that van Dusen, like Alan Galloway, is referring to *the* Liberal Theology, but what he says has relevance to the liberal tendency in general. It was not, and is not, purely intellectual in tone or intention, even though its inquisitiveness, openness and critical mindedness owe a great deal to the principles and presuppositions of the Age of Reason. For it is also characterized by:

> spiritual vitality and power—the awareness that life is more than mind, and so must religion be; its sense of linkage with the past and the wisdom of the ages; its contagious spirituality and its moral consciousness, lofty ideals, demanding obligations.[9]

Harry Emerson Fosdick claimed that the central aim of Liberal Theology was to make it possible for someone 'to be both an intelligent modern and a serious Christian',[10] and Kenneth Cauthen identified two types of liberalism—'Evangelical Liberalism' and 'Modernistic Liberalism'. He suggests that:

> the evangelical liberals can appropriately be thought of as 'serious Christians' who were searching for a theology which could be believed by 'intelligent moderns' while the modern-istic liberals can best be thought of as 'intelligent moderns' who nevertheless wished to be thought of as 'serious Christians' in some real sense.[11]

So whether a person is coming to liberalism from a position that is basically evangelical with respect to the authority of revelation and personal experience, or basically modernistic with respect to the claims of reason and modern scientific method, they are both wanting to hear both tunes and therein lies their liberalism.

Yet, to pursue van Dusen's metaphor, the child is never merely a synthesis of his or her parents. It is not possible to reduce the child to a mere compendium of parental characteristics and neither can we reduce liberalism to a mere synthesis of intellectual rigour and evangelical piety. Charles Ives did not simply hear two tunes: he heard something completely new in the coming together of those tunes. It was for him a way of listening, and if others thought he had 'his ears on wrong' that did not detract from the power and authenticity of his subsequent compositions. Likewise, liberal Christianity is at its best when it is a wide-ranging, deeply penetrating attitude of mind rather than an exercise in religio-scientific synthesis. John Habgood recalls Alec Vidler and Charles Raven as examples of how it is possible to be liberals, in these 'strikingly different ways', and he correctly observes how the synthesizing approach runs the risk of scientific imprecision on the one hand and a theological shiftiness on the other, avoiding 'the awkward questions . . . about the particularity of Christ, and sin, and human limita-tions'.[12] This latter indictment echoes H. Richard Niebuhr's merciless charge that the social gospel movement, which was itself a kind of religio-sociological synthesis dominating American Protestantism during the first half of this century, taught only how 'A God without wrath brought men without sin into a kingdom without judgement through the ministrations of a Christ without a cross'.[13] Again, Ives did not seek to harmonize two tunes and thereby run the risk of emasculating both of them, but instead to hear something completely new in their coming together.

So if Liberal Theology was 'a style of doing theology rather than a school of thought', we would want to suggest that liberalism is more an attitude of mind than a theological method—especially a synthesizing method. It is to the essential characteristics of the liberal tendency that we now turn.

Here is a fairly typical approach to defining theological liberalism:

> Liberalism in theology is that mood or cast of mind which is prepared to accept that some discovery of reason may count *against* the authority of a traditional affirmation in the body of Christian theology. One is a theological liberal if one allows autonomously functioning reason to supply arguments against traditional beliefs and if one's reformulation of Christian belief provides evidence that one has ceased to believe what has been traditionally believed by Christians.[14]

Now compare that with the following:

> . . . for me it [i.e. liberalism] represents an openness in the search for truth which I believe is profoundly necessary for the health of religion. We grow in knowledge only insofar as we are prepared to criticize what we think and know already. True knowledge is tested knowledge, just as true faith has to be sifted by doubt. . . . Openness in the search for truth also entails a positive, but again critical, approach to secular knowledge. . . . It is essentially about honesty, but an honesty rooted in what God has given us, both in revelation and in the created world.[15]

In the first extract, Stephen Sykes has chosen to define liberalism in negative terms: '. . . against . . . against . . . ceased to believe', and it is a common enough tendency to describe liberalism in terms of that to which it is opposed. On the other hand, John Habgood's definition in the second extract is conspicuously more positive in its association of liberalism with 'openness', 'growth', 'honesty', and 'the positive search for truth'. Our inclination is to side with this more positive approach, and we do so because close study of the literature and rhetoric of liberalism shows that the negative allusions are to factors that are subordinate to the essential and presiding liberal spirit.

First of all, as Habgood has stressed very strongly, liberalism entails *openness*. This openness is to truth—both in terms of where it might be found and where it might lead. It is not a prescription for indiscriminate allegiances or intellectual anarchy, and neither does it assume that liberal Christians engage with their faith without an accumulated store of knowledge and presuppositions—as Lesslie Newbigin has put it, 'it's all very well to have an open mind, but not at both ends'! The openness we speak of is openness 'to the possibility of a deeper Christian faith through modern understanding, in which the possibilities of faith are actually enriched through modern ways'.[16] In a moment we shall see how some attempts to preserve and promote this openness have proved a distraction to the essential liberal spirit, and in a later chapter we shall explore the implications of this openness for the task of Christian evangelism. Suffice it to say that anyone who has really tried to listen to—and *hear*—two tunes at once has had to have ears well and truly opened to appreciate such a miscellany of sounds.

This brings us to the second essential characteristic of the liberal tendency, which is the *commitment to listen, hear and respond* when encountering a particular context. Notice that the important distinction is made between listening and 'hearing'. This distinction has become enshrined in the rather maddening cliche 'I hear what you're saying'—but it is still none the less valid. Basically, 'listening' implies a degree of detached objectivity, while 'hearing' involves a personal and subjective engagement with 'the other'. We listen to all kinds of things in our day-to-day lives, but we probably hear only a fraction of what is communicated our way. Hearing involves an act of will and makes demands upon our limited patience and powers of concentration. It is clear that whereas most of the residents of Danbury, Connecticut, merely *listened* to the cacophony of competing bands, Charles Ives *heard* something very powerful and compelling. Thus it is a mark of liberal Christianity that it does not merely listen to the still sad music of humanity or the joyful song of creation, but actively engages with these sounds so as to hear and respond creatively. When we come to spell out the nature of a liberal approach to evangelism, we shall lay some stress on the act of responding to a particular cultural context. Such a response, though, depends upon a prior commitment to objective listening and subjective hearing if the liberal spirit is to be properly honoured. Perhaps the importance of listening *and* hearing is brought out most powerfully in accounts of encounters with Christians overseas. David Paton was a missionary in China, and in a recent volume that explores 'the future of Liberal Theology' he has decribed the point he reached in his engagement with Chinese culture and tradition. He concludes as follows:

> What all this means is . . . that we have to learn to look at other people, especially those about whom we know little or nothing, in a spirit of hopefulness. It means, secondly, that the primary task is exploration of other people's strange ideas rather than hitting them on the head with our traditions. Be it noted, however, that in our traditions other people may see in among the dross, nuggets of truth which we have not noticed until they point them out to us! Thirdly, it means that we proceed with these tasks in expectant joy, rejoicing that we are entering a strange new world in which we are enriched if we persevere expectantly.[17]

This exactly expresses that spirit of openness, listening and hearing that will characterize the liberal spirit, whether the prevailing culture is 'a strange new world' or the all too familiar world of our contemporary surroundings.

The third 'essential' relates to religious and cultural *pluralism*. At the heart of any theology of evangelism there will lie more or less explicit assumptions about those who subscribe to diverse beliefs, whether religious or secular. All too often these assumptions are not fully acknowledged, so that serious damage is done by well-meaning people in pursuit of inappropriate evangelistic strategies. The history of overseas missions is littered with the consequences of mistakes and misunderstandings resulting from failure to affirm diversity of belief as a gift to be celebrated and not an aberration to be cured. Perhaps one of those Danbury bands could have turned up the volume and drowned out the other, thus gaining some credit for having the courage of its convictions. In this case, though, Charlie Ives would have been denied access to that very special awareness that came only from hearing the two tunes together. It is commonplace these days for adherents of a particular religion to 'turn up the volume' in their attempts to drown out what they perceive to be competing claims. This not only degrades those of another persuasion, and denies to religious belief a necessary humility in relation to our knowledge of God, it also drowns out the opportunity to hear what can only be heard when diversity is not merely tolerated but positively celebrated.

Now it is true that liberals have themselves been unacceptably timid in celebrating diversity and have rested content with 'tolerance' as an ultimate virtue. This has inevitably fuelled charges of timidity with respect to gospel truth and unprincipled permissiveness in matters of morality. However, what we are promoting here is not just toleration of the other tune, but a ready acknowledgement of our need to hear it simultaneously with our own. This is necessary on essentially theological grounds because, put most simply, humans are less than God, and at the heart of liberalism is 'an intoxication with the greatness and mystery of God'.[18] It is for this reason that William Hutchinson urges upon liberals not so much a commitment to religious pluralism as a religious commitment to pluralism.[19] That is, a readiness to acknowledge as a theological necessity that our grasp of the truth as we see it must always be provisional. The culture we inhabit, and the people we encounter as products and representatives of that culture, are also likely to have a grasp on the truth—and it is in our being and belonging together that we shall move a little closer to that fullness of vision that is our common goal. Such a religious commitment to pluralism requires of us the self-confidence to express clearly the truth as we see it, but always in that spirit of humility that truly expects to be challenged and changed by the truth as perceived elsewhere.

Such a spirit demands total *honesty* and this provides us with our fourth essential characteristic. Of course, all truth-claims also claim to be honest and it would be difficult to find religious people ready to admit otherwise! But the exaggerated claims that are so often made for the sources of authority in religion, such as credal formulae, traditional practices and foundation scriptures, are extraordinarily difficult to sustain in all honesty. Enormous energy is expended in the performance of such intellectual gymnastics as are necessary to defend the credibility of Genesis and the edibility of Jonah. As Martin Camroux has written, 'Liberalism asserts that any attempt to penetrate the nature and the character of the ultimate mystery will always fall short of completeness and therefore that doctrines and creeds can only approximate to the truth, never be identical with it.' He goes on to quote Augustine's dictum that 'anything which your intellect is able to comprehend is too small to be God' and concludes that 'when we lose this truth we are on the way to that blind arrogant fanaticism which is religion's curse'.[20] Quite so, and there is now as great a need as there ever was to be honest with one another before God with respect to the fragility of our credentials.

However, it is not only required of us to exercise appropriate humility with respect to our sources of authority, but we are also bound to be honest in our encounters with the culture that surrounds us. It is not certain that phrases like 'reclaiming the high ground' are helpful to what is described as 'A Christian Response to Secularism'.[21] Neither should we be totally seduced by analyses of the relationship between the gospel and our culture that threaten to move from a timely and legitimate affirmation of Christianity as public truth towards an attempt to reinstate Christianity as *the* public truth.[22] This tendency does less than justice to the truths of God mediated through the workings of the so-called 'secular' world and is not entirely honest about the capacity of Christian thought to make sense of ultimate questions independently of the successive cultures in which it has developed through time.

By no means least, we must be honest with ourselves as we try to fathom the depths of God's love in the person and work of Christ. How often liberals have been so suspicious of overstating the divinity of Jesus that they have simply clothed him in their own humanity. Camroux recalls Dennis Nineham's story about the Baptist scholar T. R. Glover. Two Oxford dons were talking together. 'Have you read Glover's autobiography?' 'I didn't know he'd written one.' 'Oh yes, he has. It's him to the life. Only for some reason he's called it "Jesus of Nazareth".'[23] There's always the danger that what Christians have to say about Jesus tells us at least as much about them as him. This is true of all Christian discourse, but it is not always acknowledged in the anxiety to present objectively certain truths uncontaminated by the malaise of human frailty. However, we must be true to our essential humanity when making metaphysical claims that penetrate beyond the reach of deductive reason, and it is that kind of humility in the quest for truth that must characterize theological liberalism, even if it goes by default elsewhere.

Creative listening to two tunes at once is a demanding business, and it is difficult to know whether it is a gift to be nurtured or a skill that can be acquired. Either way, it entails an attitude of expectancy as new and sometimes discordant claims are made upon our credulity. Even before the dawn of the Age of Enlightenment, the claims of traditional Christianity supported by the testimony of Scripture and the authoritative teaching of the Church has been made simultaneously with the claims of human reason and experience. In many ways, these latter claims have simply added weight to the tradition as reason has been used to systematize faith, and religious experience has been cited as testimony to the truth of established authorities. At critical points, though, there has been a clash of truth-claims such as to provoke bitter conflicts between Christianity and what Schleiermacher described as its 'cultured despisers'.[24] Perhaps the mid-nineteenth century clash between Bishop Samuel Wilberforce and the young scientist T. H. Huxley over Darwin's *Origin of Species* can be equated with that moment on Danbury Main Street when the two bands met. People felt compelled to take sides with the consequent consolidation of battle lines dividing 'religion' on the one hand and 'science' on the other. We have seen how at least some of those called 'liberals' sought to demonstrate their openness, honesty and commitment to modern culture by attempting to harmonize the claims of revelation with the claims of scientific discovery. If scientific accounts of how things are, conflicted with received Christian traditions, so much the worse for the tradition. Over against them, the 'conservatives' fought to defend the edifice of traditional Christianity by reaffirming the strength of its historical foundations. If biblical narrative conflicted with the findings of scientific research, so much the worse for science. Neither camp was equipped to hear above the noise of battle the true worth of the other's tune. However, there have been those who have tried to keep their ears open to both bands, listening and hearing in such a way as to discover new richness in the plurality of sounds and rhythms. They found new spiritual depths in a salvation history stripped of its obligations to factuality and new breadth of meaning in a scientific world-view liberated from obligation to religious orthodoxy. Towards the end of this chapter we shall seek to develop this kind of understanding of the liberal spirit in relation to our encounter with modern culture, and in chapter 4 we shall spell out the evangelistic implications for this kind of Christian liberalism. First, though, we must deal with a protest.

What is all the fuss about?

Openness, honesty, creative listening, hearing and responding in a world of cultural and religious diversity—if these altogether innocuous and quite unexceptional qualities constitute liberalism, then what has all the fuss been about? For years now we have been subjected to dire warnings about a 'liberal conspiracy', with the 'liberal agenda' being foisted by the 'liberal establishment' on an unwilling Church and people. In his account of the Roman Catholic response to modernity at the end of the nineteenth century, John Kent concludes that:

> What was characteristic here was the extensiveness of 'liberal' as a pejorative term from the economic 'liberalism' of the nineteenth century to 'liberalism' in general, meaning all ideas which could be said to have stemmed from the eighteenth century Enlightenment, which had replaced the Reformation as the chief source of the modern troubles of the church.[25]

This same pejorative use of the word has also marked a good deal of Protestant polemic in the twentieth century and has been well documented by Keith Clements, who quotes a First World War publication to the effect that 'to be liberal was to be unpatriotic'.[26] We have already quoted H. Richard Niebuhr's devastating attack on the liberal theology underlying 'the social Gospel' and some would say that he was excelled only by his brother Reinhold in his critique of Christian liberalism. Add to this the charges brought by the protagonists and heirs of neo-orthodoxy on the one hand to the effect that liberalism exceeded the bounds of theological propriety, and by radicals on the other to the effect that liberals have not had the courage to push those bounds far enough, and it will be appreciated just how liberalism has suffered at the hands of detraction from all sides. Yet the most vitriolic accusations have come from those who describe themselves as traditionalists, and are sometimes referred to by others as 'the conservative backlash'. Why—if all that is being promoted is honesty, openness and creativity in the relationship between Christianity and culture?

The answer would seem to lie in the fact that attitudes find expression in words and actions, policies and programmes. For example, there have been those who, in defence of the liberal attitude they hold dear, have proved most illiberal in their approach to those of another persuasion. Consequently, the type of liberalism we are promoting here has been abandoned by resorting to all-out assaults on those who retain even the least amount of allegiance to the historicity of Scripture or to the tenets of the Apostles' Creed. Of course it can be intensely frustrating when someone only wants to listen to their tune and shows no interest in anything else, but the cause of liberalism is not best served by seeking to silence others' tunes for ever and a day—not when the essence of liberalism is that the traditionalist tune should be heard, albeit in conjunction with the melodies of modernity.

On the other hand, there can also be a tendency to promote the liberal cause by showing how traditional Christianity can be totally reinterpreted in terms of a modern philosophical theory of sociopolitical agenda. Christian existentialists have been leading exponents of this sort of theological reconstruction, as have a range of political and feminist theologians. It has also characterized certain contributions to the debate about religion and science. The problem is that it can become reductionist in effect, with Christianity incorporated without remainder into an alternative scientific political or philosophical world-view. In terms of our controlling metaphor, it is not so much that the traditionalist tune is stifled, as that it is appropriated or misappropriated and rewritten to sound like another tune.

There can be no doubt that liberal Christianity has suffered guilt by association with such attempts to show that religion is *really* a branch of psychology, sociology, anthropology, etc. The fact is, though, that the liberal tendency is put into reverse by the sponsors of reductionism. Liberalism seeks to interact creatively with these disciplines of 'the New Enlightenment', just as it has related creatively to the Age of Enlightenment that nurtured them. That is a very different thing from colluding with such disciplines in their attempts to neutralize religion by showing it to be merely a branch of the human sciences. However, it must be conceded that liberal Christianity has not found it easy to resist claims that it is a party to such collusion.

Clearly, those who believe that openness and honesty are essential Christian qualities will be alarmed at closed-mindedness that is nothing less than bigotry and at claims to certainty and absolute truth that are nothing less than dishonest. Critical-mindedness is important to liberals, but it must be that creative kind of criticism that seeks to get beneath the surface of Scriptures and dogmas in order to identify what can be affirmed with confidence. It is this same kind of creative criticism that must be applied to the claims of modernity so that liberals do not end up sacrificing traditional Christianity on the altar of a particular philosophy or scientific theory. Kenneth Surin has asserted that 'exponents of "liberal" theologies tend to accept at face value those structures of intelligibility and plausibility constitutive of modernity'.[27] If they are indeed taken 'at face value', then the critical-mindedness of liberalism has been set aside and the reductionist 'liberals' have forfeited the right to be called liberal at all.

Thus it is easy to see how over-zealousness in the cause of openness to modernity can result in the closing of minds to the claims of tradition, and uncritical commitment to the cause of hearing the messages of modernity can result in believing everything that has been heard. Much of the venom against liberalism is directed at these kinds of 'liberals', and we must constantly remind ourselves that the essentials of liberalism are not terminally affected by attack on its over-enthusiastic defenders.

It is possible to see how other attempts to articulate the liberal spirit have tended to lose that sense of critical balance that is so important to the liberal cause. We can cite the social gospel movement, which was basically concerned to remove obstacles to the free flow of the liberal spirit so that the promotion of social justice and personal freedom became crucial to the establishment of the Kingdom of God. How easy it was, though, for the 'Just Society' to become a necessary condition for the Kingdom of God, rather than a consequence of it, so that the gospel of personal responsibility, repentance and renewal tended to get lost in the rhetoric of social responsibility. Again, the New England Transcendentalists like Ralph Waldo Emerson, who epitomized the liberal spirit in so many ways, legitimately pleaded for divine revelation to be released from the limited scope of historical events and so be extended to the whole world of nature and human experience. Yet they also allowed their positive message to be tarnished by such a negative approach to historic Christianity as must seriously undermine the liberal allegiance to the God of both traditional faith and modern culture. Again, we can see how the popular liberal emphasis on tolerance was a well-intentioned attempt to affirm cultural and religious pluralism, but tended towards the excesses of 'anything goes', while much the same fate befell the prophets of existentialist and situation ethics as they sought to promote the claims of love over against law in resolving moral dilemmas. Likewise, liberal determination to uphold the cause of Christian humanism has run like a golden thread through Western culture since the eve of the Reformation, and is as vital today as ever it was—indeed, 'True Christianity is a faith with the courage to be humanist.'[28] Yet it has not always been easy to hold on to the essentially theological core of this tradition, so that some liberals have become indistinguishable from secular humanists and thus have become easy targets for traditionalist sniper-fire—as have those who have wanted to affirm a liberal commitment to Christianity as a way of life rather than a set of dogmas, and have failed to see that the two are not mutually exclusive;[29] and those who have argued for feelings as mattering more than facts and have implied that facts don't matter at all; and those who drank deeply from the wells of Enlightenment optimism that prospered with the scientific revolution, but then fell foul of those twentieth-century atrocities that poured scorn on 'the myth of progress'.

All this adds up to an acknowledgement that liberalism has been adept at scoring own goals, especially when on the attack against non-liberal obscurantism or on the defence against threats to the liberal tendency. The difficult business of listening to two tunes has given way to either the suppression of one tune or the amplification of the other. However, this must not be allowed to eclipse the legitimate claims of liberal theology to be 'the least inadequate, most credible and cogent interpretation of Christian Faith in the nineteen centuries of its history'.[30]

Both Christianity and culture

We are now in a position to discuss how liberalism contributes to an appropriate understanding of the relationship between Christianity and modern culture.

David Ford has tried to assess 'the significance of modernity for the content and method of theology' by deploying Hans Frei's theological typology:

> Imagine a line punctuated by five types of theology. At one end, the first type is simply the attempt to repeat a traditional theology or version of Christianity and see all reality in its own terms, with no recognition of the significance for it of other perspectives or of all that has happened in recent centuries. At the other extreme, the fifth type gives complete priority to some modern secular philosophy or worldview, and Christianity in its own terms is only valid insofar as it fits in with that. So parts of Christian faith and practice may be found true or acceptable, but the assessment is always made according to criteria which are external to faith and which claims superiority to it. . . .
>
> That leaves three types in between. Type two might be characterised by Anselm of Canterbury's motto 'faith, seeking understanding'. It insists that Christian identity is primary and that all other reality needs to be construed in relation to it, but also that Christianity itself needs continually to be re-thought and that theology must engage seriously with the modern world in its quest for understanding. Type three comes exactly at the middle of the line. It is a theology of correlation. It brings traditional Christian faith and understanding into dialogue with modernity, and tries to correlate the two in a wide variety of ways. It does not claim any overarching integration of Christianity and modernity – neither one that would subsume modernity within Christian terms nor one that would exhaustively present Christianity in specifically modern terms. . . . In a period of fragmentation and pluralism the

method of correlation is especially attractive as a way of keeping going a range of open dialogues. . . .

The fourth type uses a particular (or sometimes more than one) modern philosophy, conceptuality or problem as a way of integrating Christianity with an understanding of modernity. It wants to do justice to both and sees the best way of doing this to be the consistent reinterpretation of Christianity in terms of some contemporary idioms or concern.[31]

This matrix bears marked resemblance to H. Richard Niebuhr's classic study of *Christ and Culture*,[32] which also identified five approaches: Christ Against Culture; Christ Of Culture; Christ Above Culture; Christ and Culture in Paradox; Christ the Transformer of Culture. Our understanding of liberal Christianity would incline us towards Ford's Type Three and Niebuhr's Christ and Culture in Paradox. This is odd because Ford himself places liberals in Type Four and it is usual for liberals to be seen in terms of Niebuhr's Christ of Culture. However, both these approaches lean heavily towards culture calling the tune. As Niebuhr himself put it: 'Loyalty to contemporary culture has so far qualified loyalty to Christ that he has been abandoned in favour of an idol called by his name.'[33] In fact, as we have been observing above, there are deviations from the liberal spirit as we have tried to define it; but the attraction of Ford's Third Type is that it leaves the substance of tradition and modernity intact without attempting to synthesize them or to subsume one into the other—in other words, the two tunes are allowed to be heard together. It is for this reason that Paul Tillich, so clearly the 'classic modern representative' of this view,[34] has succeeded where neo-orthodoxy failed, by keeping open the contact between Christianity and modernity by affirming the integrity of both of them. It is also in the nature of a paradox that it should leave its two component parts to stand in relative tension with one another without compromise or collapsing one into the other. Niebuhr rightly draws attention to the 'vices' of dualism in so far as religion is left with nothing to say to culture and vice versa. Paradox, though, does not depend so much upon the separation of its component parts as upon the creative possibilities for faith and knowledge of holding the two together—in other words, hearing both tunes at once.

The importance of this approach lies in its refusal to define

the theological task in terms of either Christian tradition or modern culture telling the other where truth is to be found. Neither is
it primarily a matter of interpreting or inculturating the tradition
for the sake of modern ears. This is a vital task, and one that can
only be neglected at the risk of marginalization and irrelevance,
but it is merely instrumental to the primary theological task of
ensuring that the tradition has its place in the midst of a pluralist
society.

Thus we contend that the hallmarks of the liberal tendency
lead us to the following principles of engagement between
Christianity and the prevailing culture:

1. That the claims of the Christian gospel should be available to
   be heard in a pluralist society.
2. That Christian ears should be open to other truth-claims in
   such a society.
3. That the truth of God and the gospel is best served by the
   coming together of those claims in openness, honesty and
   mutual respect.

Certain implications follow from these principles.

First of all, it is the claims of *the Christian gospel* that are to
be available in a pluralist society. This ensures that liberalism is
conservative in the sense adopted by John Habgood in his
Confessions:

> The essence of conservatism, as I see it, is to treasure what is
> given by tradition, what is best from the past, and what has
> proved itself by its durability. It is to display a certain humility
> towards the things we have received and may not fully under-
> stand, and so to conserve them as potentially fruitful for the
> future.[35]

It is such treasuring of the tradition that ensures that the
critical tools adopted by liberals in their approach to Scripture
and history are devoted to the cause of preservation and not gra-
tuitous demolition. Humility towards the things we have
received is vital if liberals are to avoid the arrogance that tends
to punish the past for being the past. Hans Enzenberger, one of
post-war Germany's angry young poets, summarized a view of
tradition that has been that of many modern artists:

The minority has the majority
the dead are outvoted.[36]

It is this anti-democratic tendency in so-called liberal democra-
cies that provokes charges of high-handed hubris against the
'high priests' of modernity. Liberal theology, though, has not been
immune to this same tendency in its dealings with pre-Enlightenment Christianity. However, John Robinson was right to insist that
'a radical must be a man of roots. . . . It is my deep roots . . . that
have driven me to radical stances both in doctrine and ethics';[37]
and for all the distinctions that must be made between liberals
and radicals,[38] they are at one in their essential conservationism.
It will sometimes be the case that caution is the chief motive,
such that Christians 'feel compelled to act in cases of doubt on
the principle of the conservation of riches'.[39] However, it is
respect for tradition as 'potentially fruitful for the future' that is
really crucial here, so that there is no question of the past being
used as a bolt-hole to which retreat can be made from the critiques and complexities of the modern world. Commenting on
certain trends in the post-war film industry, Lindsay Anderson
observed that, 'The Past is no longer an inspiration, it is a
refuge',[40] and there can be little doubt that some aspects of contemporary Christianity represent nothing but a 'retreat' into
traditionalism. For others, traditional religion is used as what
Peter Berger calls 'a sacred canopy over the status quo' so that
fundamentalism becomes a way of dealing with the future on the
part of people who think that maintaining a religious identity
they are comfortable with is paramount.[41] In such cases, continuity with the past is rightly affirmed, but it is a 'handing on' of
the tradition rather than a 'handing over';[42] an undifferentiated
continuity rather than 'continuity with real differences'.[43]

Liberalism is strong on continuity with the past, in spite of
efforts to malign it otherwise, but it is a continuity that is more
than mere reiteration—it is a continuity that ensures that the
gospel is available to be *heard* in contemporary society. Those
who went in quest of the historical Jesus did so out of the conviction that the Christian gospel could only be heard in the
modern world in so far as it had been honestly subjected to the
rigours of historical criticism. Claims to immunity from such
critical analysis might ensure the gospel its own patch of high

ground, but it would be topped by an ivory tower delivering only megaphone messages to the secular surroundings. Liberalism is indeed committed to what Daniel Hardy calls 'the creative re-appropriation of the tradition',[44] but it is also committed to the creative re-presentation of the tradition in forms accessible, and therefore *available*, to modern consciousness. This must involve a degree of linguistic and cultural translation in order to accommodate the mind-set of people today, and it is widely acknowledged—even in some conservative evangelical circles— that it will also involve some reinterpretation of texts and dogmas if contact is to be kept with contemporary culture. However, it is not sufficient simply to say the same things in a new way. Liberal theology engages with successive and diverse cultures in a spirit of expectation that new treasures will emerge from the tradition as a result of such encounters. Past encounters of this kind have bequeathed much to our theological and spiritual advantage, and new encounters hold the promise of good things to come—but only if Christians are genuinely open to the claims and insights of the culture to which they have been sent or of which they are themselves a part. It is to this, our second key principle, that we now turn.

'Culture' is an 'exceptionally complex term', beginning as a noun of process—the culture of crops as in horticulture—and developing to mean the 'informing spirit' of a whole way of life on the one hand and a specific social order on the other.[45] The latter is often the material manifestation of the former, so that a 'permissive culture' may manifest itself in 'drug culture' or 'hippy culture'. In the context of studies exploring the relation-ship between religion and culture, it is generally a conflation of these emphases that is intended, so that Hugh Montefiore on behalf of 'The Gospel and Our Culture' movement speaks of 'the unconscious assumptions which underlie the thinking of a society and by which its members live their lives',[46] and Daniel Jenkins defines culture as 'a distinctive style of living based on common values'.[47]

It is now generally agreed that however culture is defined and understood, the Enlightenment has exerted, and continues to exert, a controlling influence on the development of modern cul-ture in the Western world. There is less agreement on the precise nature and extent of this influence, but we have already noticed how the Enlightenment weighs heavily on the minds of those who see it as the main cause of modernity's ills on the one hand, or the last great hope for the rescue of Christianity from antique obscurity on the other. Either way, the world could not be looked at in quite the same way again and the truth-claims of traditional Christianity could not be asserted without taking account of this 'informing spirit' that exerted such a controlling influence on the attitudes, lifestyle and values of Western society.

In other words, contemporary Christianity must have its ears open to the voices of a culture functioning under the influence of the Age of Enlightenment. This is not to say that Christianity must capitulate to those voices. That would be manifest folly in the light of the weaknesses in the world-view to which we have already alluded. It would also be a betrayal of religious truth, which is concerned with questions of meaning and value and does not need to be accurately reporting scientific data to be still in touch with reality. It does mean, though, that modern Christianity must be alert to hear what the Spirit is saying to the Churches with the expectation that the mouthpiece of the Spirit may well be the Spirit of the Age.

Finally, we contend that when the claims of the gospel are made accessible to modern ears, and Christian ears are open to the claims of modernity, then truth will have a chance to transcend the small-mindedness of religious triumphalism on the one hand and scientific imperialism on the other. Hearing the claims of the prevailing culture, Christians will find just how resourceful the gospel can be in responding to these claims; and because the response is attuned to the culture, it thus becomes possible, once again, for people to hear in their own tongues the mighty works of God. This is the essence of a liberal approach to evangelism.

Postscript

We cannot leave this account of the liberal tendency without taking note of postmodernism and post-liberalism, which have decisively influenced the method and content of recent theological studies in a so-called 'post-Enlightenment' culture.

Post-liberal theology basically represents an attempt to

reinstate the Christian tradition, and especially the biblical narrative, as a framework within which to understand the world. It clearly owes a good deal to Karl Barth, and it has been variously articulated in the writings of Hans Frei, George Lindbeck, and Stanley Hauerwas. In so far as it sees the Christian story as a reference point from which to evaluate and interpret cultural norms and assumptions, it has also found expression in the writings of Lesslie Newbigin and 'The Gospel and Our Culture' movement. It is *post*-liberal because it seeks to reaffirm the particularity of Christian tradition and truth over against the alleged universalism of Liberal Protestants, who forfeited Christian priority in favour of general religious studies.

Note that this is not 'conservative' theology in the sense of a simple return to old-time religion. The methods and conclusions of biblical criticism are taken seriously, as is the historically conditioned nature of Christian doctrine. However, the primary emphasis is laid on the givenness of the text as we have it rather than on identifying and analysing the sources that lie behind it. This emphasis is especially associated with Brevard Childs's canonical approach to the Scriptures, where the canon provides the fundamental Christian narrative that has formed the Christian community and focused its critique of non-Christian culture. Post-liberals

> insist that the biblical narratives provide the framework within which Christians understand the world. Christian theology describes how the world looks as seen from that standpoint; it does not claim to argue from some 'neutral' or 'objective' position. It pursues apologetics, therefore, only on an *ad hoc* basis, looking for common ground with a given conversation partner but not assuming some universally acceptable standard of rationality.[48]

Hans Frei took this *ad hoc* approach to the extreme of not being too concerned about how non-believers become believers, while Newbigin is much more committed to a 'logic of mission', so that 'where the church is faithful to its Lord . . . people begin to ask the question to which the Gospel is the answer'.[49]

This latter position is certainly more akin to conservative models of evangelism than most post-liberals would allow, but it does share with them the merit of being responsive, with the implication that culture has to be given a hearing even though there is no expectation that the culture will enhance the gospel in ways envisaged by the 'two-tunes' model advanced in this chapter.

The post-liberal position also owes something to postmodernism. This movement in recent theology has seriously challenged those 'overall interpretations of reality which have given many nineteenth- and twentieth-century critiques of religion their confidence and impact'.[50] For example, the sociopolitical theories of Marx offered a total view of how things are, and how they should be, with religion eliminated from the resulting materialist solutions. Freud makes similar claims for his analytical psychology, so that Christian perspectives on reality were effectively suppressed. Postmodernism has adopted a 'hermeneutic of suspicion' towards such 'theories of everything', so that Christianity can breathe freely again after a period of ideological suffocation.

However, other aspects of postmodernism tend to take away from Christianity with one hand what they might have given with the other. At least Kant had affirmed the possibility of reality being accessible to human consciousness and the possibility of God being available to human reason—albeit subjectively rather than according to the objective criteria of pre-Enlightenment metaphysics. Now postmodernists such as Derrida and Foucault call into question the possibility of human beings getting in touch with 'reality' at all. Truth-claims are basically linguistic constructs, so that it is possible to talk *about talk about God,* but it is not possible to talk *about God*—not even in the subjectivist categories of modernism.

If we have to trade labels, then what we are promoting here could be described as liberal postmodernism! That is, we want to join with postmodernists in challenging the 'closed book' mentality that 'licenses a single, restricted interpretative paradigm within which we must operate if one wishes to enjoy the rewards that are on offer'.[51] On the other hand, we want to lose none of the fruits of biblical and historical criticism that have been harvested by liberal studies of the Christian tradition over two centuries.

We need to balance the search for original intentions and modern responses if the Bible is to be not only 'the site of a proliferation of meanings',[52] but also a focus of continuity with the origins of Christianity and the chroniclers of those origins.[53]

However, whether the prevailing culture is Enlightenment or post-Enlightenment, or something in between, it remains true that the claims of culture must be taken seriously if the claims of tradition are to be taken seriously in their turn. That is crucial to our understanding of the liberal tendency and its application to the call to evangelism.

Notes

1. See Frank R. Rossiter, *Charles Ives and His America*. Gollancz 1976, pp. 15–16.
2. Charles B. Ives, *Memos*, ed. John Kirkpatrick. New York, V. W. Norton, 1972, p. 71.
3. Allan D. Galloway, in P. Avis, ed., *The Science of Theology*. Marshall Pickering 1986, p. 294.
4. J. Réville, *Liberal Christianity*. London 1903, p. 7.
5. See Robert S. Michaelsen and Wade Clark Roof, eds, *Liberal Protestantism*. New York, Pilgrim Press, 1986.
6. See Bernard M. G. Reardon, *Liberal Protestantism*. A & C Black 1968, p. 10.
7. John Habgood, *Confessions of a Conservative Liberal*. SPCK 1988, p. 2. See also, C. Marsh, *Questioning Evangelism*, Grove Books 1993, p. 4.
8. H. P. van Dusen, *The Vindication of Liberal Theology*. New York, Scribner's 1963, p. 21.
9. Ibid., p. 22.
10. H. E. Fosdick, *The Living of these Days*. New York, Harper & Row, 1956, p. vii.
11. Kenneth Cauthen, *The Impact of American Religious Liberalism*. Harper & Row 1962, pp. 27, 29. See also van Dusen, *The Vindication of Liberal Theology*, pp. 24–5.
12. John Habgood, in D. W. Hardy and P. H. Sedgwick, eds, *The Weight of Glory*. T. & T. Clark 1991, pp. 5f. See also, J. Habgood, *Making Sense*. SPCK 1993, pp. 197–207.
13. H. Richard Niebuhr, *The Kingdom of God in America*. New York, Harper & Row, 1937, p. 191.
14. S. W. Sykes, *Christian Theology Today*. Mowbray 1971, p. 12.
15. Habgood, *Confessions*, p. 2. For a commendation of Habgood's brand of liberalism by a conservative critic, see Alister McGrath, *The Renewal of Anglicanism*, SPCK 1993, pp. 123–4.
16. D. W. Hardy, in Hardy and Sedgwick, eds, *The Weight of Glory*, p. 300.

17. David Paton, in Hardy and Sedgwick, eds, *The Weight of Glory*, p. 297.
18. Habgood, in Hardy and Sedgwick, eds, *The Weight of Glory*, p. 12.
19. William R. Hutchinson, 'Past Imperfect: History and the Prospect for Liberalism', in Michaelsen and Roof, *Liberal Protestantism*, p. 79.
20. M. Camroux, 'The Case for Liberal Theology', *The Expository Times*, 1992, (vol. 103) p. 170.
21. H. Montefiore, *Re-claiming the High Ground.* Macmillan 1990.
22. See, for example, Lesslie Newbigin, *The Gospel in a Pluralist Society.* SPCK 1989, and H. Montefiore, ed., *The Gospel and Contemporary Culture.* Mowbray 1992.
23. Camroux, 'The Case for Liberal Theology', p. 169.
24. For a lively account of these controversies in England in the twentieth century, see Keith W. Clements, *Lovers of Discord.* SPCK 1988.
25. John Kent, *The Unacceptable Face: The Modern Church in the Eyes of the Historian.* SCM Press 1987, p. 24.
26. Clements, *Lovers of Discord*, pp. 72–3.
27. David F. Ford, ed., *The Modern Theologians,* vol. II. Basil Blackwell 1989, p. 111.
28. Haddon Willmer, in *20/20 Visions.* SPCK 1992, p. 152. See also Stephen Platten, 'Reclaiming Christian Humanism', *Crucible*, October–December 1991, pp. 179–88.
29. See Donald E. Miller, *The Case for Liberal Christianity.* SCM 1981.
30. van Dusen, *The Vindication of Liberal Theology*, p. 17.
31. Ford, ed., *The Modern Theologians*, vol. II, pp. 2–4.
32. H. Richard Niebuhr, *Christ and Culture.* Faber & Faber 1952.
33. Niebuhr, *The Kingdom of God in America*, p. 118.
34. Ford, ed., *The Modern Theologians*, vol. II, p. 3.
35. Habgood, *Confessions*, pp. 2–3.
36. Patrick Bridgwater, ed., *Twentieth-century German Verse.* Penguin.
37. Eric James, *A Life of Bishop John A. T. Robinson.* Fount 1987, pp. 113 and 211.
38. See John Macquarrie, *Thinking About God.* SCM Press 1975, chapter 6, and Dorothee Solle, *Thinking About God.* SCM Press 1990, chapter 2.
39. Stephen Sykes, *Christian Theology Today.* Mowbray 1971, p. 40.
40. Quoted in Angus Calder, *The Myth of the Blitz.* Jonathan Cape 1991, p. 263.
41. See Martin Marty and A. Scott Appleby, *Fundamentalism Observed.* University of Chicago Press 1992.
42. Christopher Moody, 'Apostolicity and the Call of the Kingdom', *Theology*, March–April 1991, p. 86.
43. van Dusen, *The Vindication of Liberal Theology*, p. 89.
44. Hardy, in Hardy and Sedgwick, eds, *The Weight of Glory*, p. 301.
45. Raymond Williams, *Culture.* Fontana 1981, pp. 10–12.
46. Montefiore, ed., *The Gospel and Contemporary Culture*, p. 2.

47. Alan Richardson and John Bowden, eds, *A New-Dictionary of Christian Theology*. SCM Press 1983, p. 137.
48. William C. Placher, 'Post-liberal Theology', in Ford, ed., *The Modern Theologians*, vol. II, p. 117.
49. Newbigin, *The Gospel in a Pluralist Society*, p. 119.
50. Ford, ed., *The Modern Theologians*, vol. II, p. 292.
51. Francis Watson, ed., *The Open Text*. SCM Press 1993, p. 3.
52. Ibid.
53. See pages 72–7 in this volume: 'A word for all seasons'.

3

Flexible Response

It would be totally out of character for a liberal approach to evangelism to be in open competition with other evangelistic strategies. Certainly, the liberal approach will differ from other approaches and will be marked by characteristics that distinctively reflect the marks of liberalism as detailed in the previous chapter. These marks, though, simply mean that there must be room for liberals to tolerate a range of approaches to the evangelistic task in the light of developments in culture, society and individual circumstances.

This point about being a different and distinctive mode of evangelism rather than a prescribed and definitive one needs to be emphasized, because liberalism often displays a contrary tendency to be unbearably intolerant of others while at the same time preaching tolerance as one of the first principles of authentic Christianity. The almost totalitarian intolerance by liberals is legendary in the annals of religious observance. Once the enemy has been identified as obscurantism or fundamentalism or mindless conservatism, then a policy of blanket bombing the enemy into ideological oblivion is promoted. If bits of the Bible are declared not 'true' in one sense of the word, then none of it is allowed to be 'true' in any sense of the word. If the traditional teachings and practices of the Church are unacceptable in certain particulars, then the very pastness of the past is enough to condemn it in every particular. If a branch of Christendom has been exposed for its espousal of a now discredited creed or code of conduct, then that branch is to be summarily cut off and cast aside for the sake of sound and acceptable Christianity.

Yet what has this kind of knee-jerk liberalism got to do with that honesty, openness and responsiveness that we have identified as essential characteristics of the liberal tendency? The fact is that 'liberals' can be just as passionate and committed in their pursuit of truth and righteousness as any of those who take a contrary point of view. Even though liberals are caricatured as cowards nailing their colours to the fence, or as ditherers standing in the middle of the road waiting to be struck by the traffic going both ways, the fact is that they are more justly condemned for stealing the clothes of those whose sealed systems of tolerable truth and sanctioned morality they profess to deplore. Of course, there is a sense in which liberals are in a no-win situation —destined to be attacked for tolerating all-comers on the one hand and for blood-curdling indignation on the other. This ambivalence, though, is to be bravely borne in so far as such tolerance is intellectually honest and such indignation is tempered by righteousness. For example, there can be no case for liberals tolerating the oppression of the weak by the strong or the suppression of the truth by the beneficiaries of falsehoods. But neither can liberals justify oppressing the oppressor at the expense of their dignity or suppressing the falsehoods at the expense of intellectual humility. All this adds up to saying that a liberal approach to evangelism must be consistent with the controlling criteria of the liberal tendency, and this must mean that it will be prepared to stand as one approach among many.

In fact, even to get as far as lining up on the same start-line with what might be described as mainstream approaches to evangelism will be something of an achievement. Most of the literature arising out of the Decade of Evangelism provides little comfort for those seeking to promote a liberal contribution to the cause. This is basically because the controlling principle of the Decade is 'We have a Gospel to Proclaim', and the assumption is that this gospel is by way of being a revealed set of truths available to be preached and proclaimed to all who have ears to hear. Certainly there is an assumed need for this gospel to be presented in ways appropriate to cultural contexts and individual needs, but these are consistently treated as matters of presentation rather than substance. The gift may be wrapped in various ways to suit the recipient, but the givenness of the gospel remains essentially non-negotiable.[1] There is little to indicate that the gospel may itself be relative to the recipient or flexible in its responsiveness to the particulars of place, time and circumstance.

Yet it is precisely because a liberal approach to evangelism starts from the givenness of the situation rather than the givenness of the gospel that it needs to take its place alongside the mainstream approaches in order to ensure that the good news of liberal Christianity contributes to a varied yet balanced schedule of evangelistic strategies.

Furthermore, and perhaps most important of all, there is a significantly large body of committed Christians who are already operating such a strategy, or who are peculiarly well equipped to promote such a strategy, but who feel themselves bypassed by an evangelistic band-wagon. They are no less aware than anyone else of their vocation to lead people into Christian discipleship, but they simply cannot operate with the assumptions underlying typical calls and campaigns to evangelize our contemporary culture. These are not washed-up intellectuals who have sold out to the spirit of the age; neither are they timid pew-fodder lacking courage or commitment to carry their convictions into the lives of those around them. They are valued and valuable members of the body of Christ who have an instinct for the resourcefulness of the gospel and a concern to respond with carefulness and sensitivity to the felt needs of a changing world. They honestly seek to face the realities of how things are, and are open to the possibility that how things are might actually help us to see more clearly how the gospel would have them be—and to the possibility that a gospel resourced by engagement with human personality and culture might yet rescue truth from the clutches of false certainty and freely irrigate those 'dykes of love in a loveless world' that Bishop John Robinson described some thirty years ago. In short, they are people who are responding flexibly to the situations in which they find themselves and they deserve to have their approach acknowledged and affirmed alongside others as evangelism takes its rightful place as the first claim on Christian energy and enterprise in this and every decade.

It is not at all easy to convince traditionalists, radicals and liberals that they need one another and are essentially interdependent. A prolonged correspondence with a conservative evangelical colleague did actually get to the point where he conceded that I was sincere in my acknowledgement that I needed him to hold and defend the base camp of traditional Christianity if I was to feel free to strike out over the horizon to explore new frontiers of faith and spirituality. He was not, though, prepared to make the reciprocal acknowledgement that he needed liberal-minded adventurers to reconnoitre the new worlds developing beyond the frontiers of past knowledge and present experience if his base-camp was not to become a frozen and fossilized monument to a venture of faith that fatally lost its nerve. Yet the much-heralded drift of Christianity into a sectarian side-show or a fundamentalist ghetto will only be halted when we all acknowledge—conservatives and liberals alike—that the gospel we all treasure needs not only to be guarded, but also to be handed over to new generations of seekers after meaning and truth. Note that, as Christopher Moody[2] has pointed out, to hand over the gospel means more than to simply hand it on in an unchanged and changeless tradition. To hand it over means to entrust it to a myriad of as yet unknown cultures and communities that *may* abuse and defuse it—or perhaps discover new treasure long hidden even from the eyes of the faithful in days gone by. The faithful guardians of the gospel base-camp and the equally faithful, though sometimes foolhardy, frontiersmen need each other if we really believe that Christ has not only come, but comes again and again. That is why a liberal approach to evangelism can never claim to be *the* approach to evangelism; and that is why an evangelistic programme that lacks the liberal approach is sadly deficient and fundamentally flawed.

The liberal approach to evangelism

Towards the end of the previous chapter, we saw how the hallmarks of the liberal tendency implied three principles of engagement between Christianity and the prevailing culture.[3] We are now in a position to explore how those principles of engagement translate into three basic principles for liberal evangelism:

1. It puts hearing before speaking.
2. It expects what has been heard to influence not only *communication* of the gospel, but also its *content*. Encounters with various cultures and individuals reveal gospel claims in a new light and uncover gospel truths as yet unrealized and unacknowledged.
3. It encourages evangelistic responses that are specific, selective and original.

We shall develop each of these principles in turn.

Hearing before speaking

This will come as no surprise in the light of all that has been said about the essential marks of the liberal tendency. All too often, evangelism has acquired a bad name because it has felt like Christianity's contribution to megaphone diplomacy! Evangelists are likely to be prized and praised more for their silver tongues than their listening ears. Oratorical skills seem to matter more than listening skills and verbal persuasiveness more than pastoral sensitivity. The microphone matters more than the ear-piece—the transmitter more than the sensitive receiver. Yet what a far cry this is from the responsiveness of Jesus as portrayed in most of the gospel accounts of his preaching and teaching ministry. Notice how often 'he answered and said'—and it is significant that his so-called 'sermons' are usually seen as literary constructs largely because they do not correspond with his less declamatory and more ideological encounters with groups and individuals. Furthermore, his responses are generally tailored to the particular circumstances of those who come to him for a healing—or simply a hearing. The deaf-mute is given the word *ephphatha* to read on his lips and the couple on the Emmaus road feel their personal anxieties and sorrows met with heart-warming persuasiveness. He listened before speaking or acting, and we sense that the power of speech was the last of his powers to be pressed into service. Yet we have turned this evangelistic strategy on its head; and it is no use protesting that St Paul set the trend, because most of the words attributed to him in the New Testament—whether they be sermons or epistles—must be contextualized as responses to what he had seen, heard and read. For all the virtues and undoubted effectiveness of powerful proclamation, we must be sure to honour this New Testament witness to listening and hearing as preconditions for evangelization.

Of course, it might be protested that modern mass-appeal evangelists are notoriously good listeners picking up the nuances of language and expression in contemporary culture so as to press the right buttons and elicit the desired response. The point, though, is that this kind of listening is directed towards the acquisition of a language with which to communicate the message; and it is not expected to impact seriously upon the message itself—which is deemed to be essentially non-negotiable. In this liberal approach to evangelism we are wanting to say that what is heard and sensed and felt by faculties attuned to the temper and tone of a prevailing culture is not only grist to the communications mill, but is also exerting a legitimate influence on the content of the gospel we then seek to proclaim. We shall be dealing further with this first principle when we develop some practical examples of this approach in action in the next chapter. First, though, we must expound more fully the contention that hearing before speaking affects what we say and not just the way that we say it—the second of our principles.

Speaking as responding

The impact of Vincent Donovan's *Christianity Rediscovered*[4] has been profound and persistent. First published in 1978, it has been read and revered by a significant ecumenical cross-section of clergy and laity in Europe and North America. The book arose out of Donovan's missionary experience as a Roman Catholic priest among the Masai people of East Africa. He describes how he became frustrated by the chronic inappropriateness of the mission methods advocated by his Church and enshrined in cumbersome structures and institutions. He rebels against the imposition of Western culture upon the people of Africa and begins again with an approach that is close to what would now be called 'inculturation'. The gospel seed had to be given time to grow in the soil of Masai culture, so that in due course it could be accepted and 'owned' in culturally appropriate ways. The impact of the book is significant because it clearly struck chords with those who were becoming anxious about the mismatch between established evangelistic methods and prevailing culture—not only in Africa and Asia, but also in the so-called 'developed' cultures of the northern hemisphere. The social and intellectual upheavals of the 1960s gave voice to a growing sense of unease at the cultural triumphalism of much overseas missionary activity in the recent past. This, in turn, gave encouragement to the case for indigenous culture to be taken seriously as the legitimate bearer of gospel truths. Hitherto, it had seemed that acceptance of the Christian creed implied a necessary acceptance of the culture of Christendom—with disastrous consequences for the culture and customs of ancient and sophisticated societies throughout the world. So-called 'home missions' were also influenced by this trend as it became increasingly necessary to study and evaluate our own culture as a vital element in 'pre-evangelism'.

All this was fine as far as it went and Donovan's book continues to have value as an enduring challenge to that cultural imperialism that has so often tainted Christian mission and evangelism. But *Christianity Rediscovered* stops well short of that liberal approach to evangelism that we are seeking to promote in these pages. Certainly Donovan makes a vital contribution to the liberal cause when he asserts that 'an evangelist . . . must respect the culture of a people, not destroy it'.[5] He movingly demonstrates a readiness to live with a people and to internalize their values and visions before trying to present the gospel to them. However, for Donovan, the gospel remains a mere matter of translation. He assumes that the gospel is 'a supracultural, unchanging message of good news',[6] even if the Church itself is culture-specific. While this is a fairly liberal position for a Roman Catholic to adopt, it still stops short of acknowledging that new facets of the gospel may be revealed by encounter with other cultures and, to that extent, it is changed. Donovan confesses that 'not one week would go by without some surprising rejoinder or reaction or revelation from these Masai' as he proceeded to 'mention a religious theme or thought and ask to hear their opinion on it'. But he goes on: 'then I would tell them what I believed on the same subject'.[7] There is no suggestion that the 'revelation from these Masai' or what he heard when he asked their opinion materially affected the beliefs he held, even if what he heard did affect the way he expressed his beliefs. Likewise, I sense that the main reason for including studies in sociology and human psychology in modern programmes of theological education is to facilitate communication with the prevailing culture rather than to enable new insights into the gospel itself, which can then be reflected back to that culture as a form of appropriate evangelism. The fact of the matter is that Donovan *did* gain powerful new insights into the nature of sacraments, community and leadership as a result of his encounter with the Masai. In addition, the negative status of women in Masai society helped Donovan to a new appreciation of the gospel's positive contribution on this subject, which he was then able to reflect back so that a group of teenage girls told him privately 'that the [good news] . . . I talked about so constantly, was really good news for them'.[8]

Perhaps this matter of the changing place of women in society is as powerful an example as any of how listening to and reading the sounds and signs of the times actually changes the gospel we proclaim. For many of us, the extraordinary increase in the activity of women in theology and biblical studies over recent years has provided, quite literally, a revelation. We have seen things in Scripture that we had not seen before—and would almost certainly never have seen if we had remained dependent on masculine perspectives. We have discerned in traditional teachings aspects of God long-hidden from view in a predominantly patriarchal culture. Much the same can be said with regard to the insights of liberation theologians, who have not simply helped us to communicate with the poor and oppressed, but have actually revealed to us a gospel 'biased to the poor' to a degree unimagined by the cultures of capititalism and economic imperialism. On a more one-to-one basis, the principles and practices of the human sciences have done far more than simply provide us with new and relevant categories with which to communicate the gospel. As Wesley Carr has shown in *The Pastor as Theologian*,[9] they have also furnished us with new keys for unlocking gospel truths revealed by, and to, the psychoanalytic culture of contemporary society.

This is not to say that the gospel is thereby reduced to psychology or sociology or cultural studies. This is the cry that always goes up whenever it is suggested that Christians have anything to learn from politics or feminism. Surely it is this fear of reductionism that has blinded us to the positive insights and revelations that can be ours if only we will be so confident in the resourcefulness of our gospel as to acknowledge that these resources may actually be made real to us by our open engagement with so-called secular society. To listen to those around us, to hear what they are saying to us and to allow their voice to impact on our gospel in surprising and creative ways, must be a sign of confidence in the infinite resources of God. So long as we are busy protecting Christianity against the taint of cultural conditioning and the charge of psycho-social reductionism, we are failing to discover and share those treasures old and new that contemporary culture can help us to discover and that contemporary culture needs to hear proclaimed as good news for our times. In short, hearing two tunes at once does not necessarily result in one tune being reduced to the other. Rather, it can enable a new tune to be heard that is gospel truth for this person or these people in this culture at this time. When we speak of 'the Christian gospel' or 'the Christian message', it is in terms of this rich seam of inexhaustible riches, some yet to be discovered, rather than in terms of a defined and predetermined deposit of truths already revealed and ready-to-wear. This leads conveniently into the third principle.

Responding in kind

Evangelistic responses should be culturally and personally *specific*. This follows from our contention that a liberal approach to sharing the good news of God will tend to begin with the givenness of a context rather than with the givenness of the gospel itself. This is not in any way to negate the initiative of God in creation and redemption or to belittle the 'scandal of particularity' that confronts humanity with the challenge of God uniquely incarnate in the first-century Palestinian Jesus of Nazareth. The events at the heart of the gospel remain events specifically placed in space and time. We are wanting, though, to say that the full profundity and significance of the Christ event will not be perceived and shared so long as we begin over and over again with the givenness of the New Testament text and/or the givenness of the events underlying the text. Rather, we shall want to begin by interrogating the text with questions posed by successive cultural contexts and individual circumstances. We will want to see how a multi-faceted gospel can be illuminated from numerous points of view, thus enabling the good news to be reflected in new and diverse ways. Again, we shall develop the practical implications of this approach in a subsequent chapter. Suffice it here to offer just one example of what this means with respect to the meaning of the cross and its enduring significance.

It is commonplace to observe that of all the doctrines central to the Christian gospel, the meaning of Christ's death is a matter about which the Church has been most reluctant to formulate a dogmatic definition. The New Testament itself bristles with an extraordinary range of images, each of which presents a particular dimension of what it means to say that Christ died for 'our sins' (1 Corinthians 15.3). The basic framework of the message remains constant: God and humanity were meant to be *at one*; human sin put them *at odds*; someone must be *at pains* so that the intended *at-one-ment* can be restored. How all this happens is expressed through such images as deliverance, redemption, justification, propitiation, reconciliation, sacrifice and so on. A full account of the New Testament understanding of the death of Christ is a major and kaleidoscopic undertaking, especially when the attempt is made to link the images to the contexts and circumstances of various groups and individuals all asking what it might mean to say that Jesus died for them.

This tendency to develop images of atonement appropriate to times and places persists throughout the history of the Christian Church. For example, the Hellenistic world relished the battle between light and darkness and was moved by the good news of Jesus, the light of the world, entering the dark places of sin and death, and achieving a victory in which all can share. Others felt their lives held in the grip of a personal devil, who Jesus challenged and conquered through death and resurrection so that the faithful might be freed for the service of God. In the medieval world, the death of Christ came to be seen as an act of chivalry, making satisfaction for God's honour tarnished through disobedience. At the Reformation, society was marked by a strong sense of legal propriety such that a punishment needed to be borne in expiation of a crime. Thus the death of Christ was proclaimed as the punishment borne by God himself to expiate the sins of fallen humanity. By the nineteenth century, the impact of the Enlightenment was felt strongly throughout Europe, with its emphasis on individual responsibility and interpersonal relationships. Salvation was now felt to be a matter of morality, with Christ dying for our example rather than in our stead. In this century, the traumas of global warfare and calculated genocide have forced Christians to face up to the viability of faith in a God of love in the midst of such unmitigated evil. So Jesus on the cross becomes the focus of God's identification with suffering humanity, or the sign of God's ultimate assumption of responsibility for the way things are. In an important recent study in atonement theory, John Moses has captured the current taste for 'holism' and has persuasively shown its relevance to our understanding of the cross.[10]

Of course, these different understandings of Christ's death have often existed alongside one another—indeed, once a particular image has come into play it has tended to remain in play whatever new 'theories' of the atonement may subsequently arise. It is clear, though, that these images owe a great deal to the various social contexts and human situations that gave rise to them. The engagement of theologians of successive generations with the questions, assumptions and thought-forms of their respective worlds has enabled them to take the terse New Testament assertion that Christ died 'for us' and to turn it into good news for their time and place. They have done this, not by compromising the gospel or rendering it culturally relative, but by tapping the resourcefulness of what has been handed over to them and proclaiming it in fresh and appropriate ways. It is more than a matter of mere presentation. They have actually found new things to say—not just new ways of saying the same things. These new things have always been there, so that they are discovered not invented. However, the discovery is consequent upon a prior listening to the sounds and assumptions of society and the brave cross-examination of Jesus' death in the light of what has been felt and heard. We in our generation continue to try to meet the challenge to show and share what it might mean for Christ to have died for our particular culture and for individual members of it. This concentration on context as essential to the formulation of a gospel for our times is a crucial element in a liberal approach to evangelism.

Now if evangelism needs to be specific to given circumstances and situations, then it has also to be *selective* in its use of the resources handed over to this generation of Christians by those who have preceded us. No doubt there will be objections raised against such selectivity, but at least a liberal who positively exploits the range of resources available for evangelistic purposes is being more honest than those who trumpet the inerrancy of Scripture, but then speak and act on the assumption that some bits are more inerrant than others! It is the difference between the truth and validity of Scripture being promoted *because of*, rather than *in spite of*, its literary variety and uneven theological quality. The Bible is not so much a source book as a resource book, available to be plundered for its wealth of discovered and as yet undiscovered treasures. So long as we are for ever going back to the Bible in terms of going back to a source, we are bound to become obsessive about its intrinsic provenance and authority. But when we apply ourselves to drawing upon the resources of the Bible in the context of our engagement with a changing world, then we discover the true measure of its worth as a tool for evangelism. Let us see what it might mean for us to be selective in our evangelistic use of the resources available to us in Bible and tradition.

Near to the Statue of Liberty in the waters around New York is Ellis Island, where tens of thousands of European immigrants were processed prior to their admission to the United States or their return from whence they came. It is now a museum full of evocative echoes that remind us of a bitter-sweet episode in the growth of a great nation. Among the exhibits is a cartoon depicting twenty or so portraits of George Washington. Each is recognizably the same father of the nation, yet each is portrayed according to the characteristics of a particular immigrant nationality—Russian, Italian, Hungarian, Spanish and so on. The cartoon illustrates how there is a George Washington for every new American, whatever their nationality or ethnic origin. Surely as much and more can be said for Jesus, whose many 'faces' have already been depicted and celebrated by countless works of art throughout the ages and around the world. Indeed, a satisfying theological 'party game' is to display a range of reproductions portraying different faces of Christ around a room and invite participants to match each face with one of a choice of captions—teacher, healer, Son of Man, Son of God, judge, friend, shepherd, King, etc. The effect of this exercise is to bring home not only the reality of the fact that we have four distinctive portraits of Jesus in the respective Gospels, but that within each of those Gospels other faces are to be found comforting, challenging, disturbing and befriending us according to need and circumstance. Paul Tillich observed that 'there can be only one Christ, but he must be the Christ for everyone' and it is in the various faces Christ shows to the world that each person in every culture can find Christ for themselves.

The many faces of Christ provide many criteria with which to evaluate the myriad values and claims promoted in a pluralistic society. The many faces of Christ also provide many reasons to expect that such pluralism will be met by a Christ who is 'for everyone'—God is God *of* everyone, and God is *for* everyone in Christ. That is what is meant by the essentially Christocentric thrust of liberal theology.[11]

The incarnational 'big bang' has issued in an expanding universe of Christological truth that can never be exhausted, or exhaustively defined, so long as there are Christ-centred people ready to respond to a Christ-hungry world with the infinite resources of a Christ-like God. Attempts to pin down the exact nature of Jesus' personhood will always tend to reduce the repertoire of his responses to the needs of a changed and ever-changing world. To acknowledge and celebrate that repertoire of responses is to affirm that in the faces of Jesus there is a face for all, and that for all who come face to face with Jesus there is a person of Christ known as if for the very first time—and there, in the resourcefulness and in the response, lies the only uniqueness that really matters.

Many recent writings have explored the ways in which Jesus has been portrayed at different times in disparate cultural contexts. Jaroslav Pelikan has traced *Jesus through the Centuries*,[12] revealing, among many others, Jesus the Rabbi, the Light of the Gentiles, the King of Kings, the Cosmic Christ, the Monk, the Universal Man, the Liberator, the Prince of Peace. John Bowden has identified 'the Kaleidoscopic Christ' (in *Jesus: The Unanswered Questions*[13]) and he draws on a French series entitled *Jesus depuis Jesus*, which covers, among others, the Manichaean Jesus, the Christ of the Barbarians, the Imperial Christ, the Slavonic Christ, the Scientific Christ and the Colonial Jesus. In addition, Robert J. Schrieter has given us *Faces of Jesus in Africa*,[14] and Anton Wessels has described perceptions and portrayals of Jesus in non-European cultures.[15] Bowden suggests that 'the images of Christ are . . . too variegated, too contradictory, too much coloured by the varieties of culturally-conditioned Christianity to serve as any guideline that can usefully be adopted',[16] and this must be true in so far as we are seeking to arrive at a definitive portrait and characterization corresponding with a Jesus of history. Once, though, we accept that the Gospels are tools of evangelism rather than records of historical actuality, we can appreciate the richness of the resources available to us as we match familiar faces of Jesus with the people and situations we encounter, and discover new and unfamiliar faces of Jesus in our engagement with new worlds of knowledge and meaning.

If one of our primary tasks in evangelism is to ask 'What does it mean for Christ to have died for this particular culture and for individual members of it?', then a second task must be to identify, and respond with, a face of Christ that meets that culture and person face to face. The gospel tradition is full of possibilities, and we are right to be selective in our drawing upon this tradition in our quest to ensure that the Christ who is for everyone is indeed the Christ who is for this one, here and now.

By no means least, a third dimension is entailed by the sheer fecundity of the gospel tradition as a resource for faith and faith-sharing. As John Macquarrie has observed: 'In any given historical situation, some aspects of the Gospel will come into focus as specially related to the needs of that situation. Every generation has to discover and re-discover the Gospel'.[17] More recently, Anton Wessels has concluded, as a result of his study of images of Jesus in a variety of cultures, that 'Not only does Christ change and transform other cultures, but it is also true that other cultures and religions bring out features in the face of Christ which had not been revealed before.'[18]

Thus a liberal approach to evangelism entails: (i) a requirement to hear, mark, learn and understand societies and persons within society; (ii) a determination to read, mark, learn and inwardly digest the tradition handed to us, so that we may draw freely on its resources for making Christ known to each succeeding generation, and (iii) a readiness to be surprised and challenged by new faces of Christ manifested at the interface between tradition and contemporary existence.

Certainly such an approach is not without its risks. Will one ever get beyond the listening stage and actually move on to proclamation? Will our selectivity be such as to collude so completely with our context that we fail seriously to challenge it—will we comfort the disturbed, but never disturb the comfortable? Will the variety of responses we make in our commitment to flexibility be such as to substitute shifting sands for firm foundations—if for everyone there is a Christ, then where is

Tillich's Christ who is for everyone? And when we claim to discern new images of Jesus in our contacts with contemporary culture, is it not fair to assume that culture has simply made him according to its own likeness? These risks are real and must be honestly acknowledged by those seeking to give liberalism an evangelistic dimension, but they are by no means fatal to the enterprise—hearing does not have to be at the expense of responding; selectivity does not have to be collusive; flexibility does have to be without consistency; new faces of Christ do not have to be the faces of Narcissus. As with all evangelistic strategies, there are pitfalls and excesses that have to be avoided. We have already observed that other approaches to evangelism are liable to succumb to temptations that are equally as real as those identified with the approach we are promoting here. Coercion, manipulation, escapism, triumphalism and uncritical dogmatism are unacceptable aspects of evangelism, but who will deny that they are ever-present risks in much mainstream missionary activity?

Yet risks have to be taken because Christians are not called to play safe when it comes to sharing the good news of God in Christ. Paul writes: 'For I received from the Lord what I also delivered to you, that the Lord Jesus on the night when he was betrayed took bread . . .' (1 Corinthians 11.23). The same Greek verb is used for 'delivered' and 'betrayed'. We cannot always be too sure whether we are doing the one thing or the other when we seek to 'hand over' the gospel to new disciples. How often do we betray Christ when we are trying to convey him—how often do we corrupt the gospel in our efforts to make it real? Our God, though, is a risk-taking God—what colossal risks are involved in creation and incarnation!—and we must be a risk-taking people if we are to be truly God's people. Flexible response is a risky strategy, but to that extent it is a gospel-strategy and is evangelistic in all the best senses of the word.

Notes

1. The range of 'Decade' literature is enormous, and we must beware of unfair generalizations. However, it remains true that while Philip King's *Making Christ Known: A Decade Handbook* (CIO 1992) examines 'some helpful and sensitive approaches to evangelism' (p. 3) that

could well include the principles of liberal evangelism, and Nigel McCulloch acknowledges 'that there is nothing so complicated as trying to pass on the simple message of God's love' (*A Gospel to Proclaim*. Darton, Longman & Todd 1992, p. xi), the writings of Michael Green and Michael Marshall have been less accommodating in their recommendations. See, for example, M. Marshall, *The Gospel Connection* (Darton, Longman & Todd 1991). The aggressiveness of many of the methods and metaphors offers little scope for any sort of open, attentive and responsive approach to the evangelistic task. It is testimony to the Archbishop of Canterbury's breadth of commitment to the Decade that he has furnished a foreword to each of the books cited in this note.

2. Christopher Moody, 'Apostolicity and the Call of the Kingdom', *Theology*, March 1991, p. 86.
3. See above, p. 31.
4. Vincent J. Donovan, *Christianity Rediscovered*. SCM Press 1992.
5. Ibid., p. 30.
6. Ibid., p. 48.
7. Ibid., p. 41.
8. Ibid., p. 121.
9. Wesley Carr, *The Pastor as Theologian*. SPCK 1989.
10. John Moses, *The Sacrifice of God*. Canterbury Press 1993.
11. See above, pp. 8–9.
12. Jaroslav Pelikan, *Jesus through the Centuries*. Yale 1985.
13. John Bowden, *Jesus: The Unanswered Questions*. SCM Press 1988.
14. Robert J. Schrieter, *Faces of Jesus in Africa*. SCM Press 1991.
15. Anton Wessels, *Images of Jesus*. SCM Press 1990.
16. Bowden, *Jesus: The Unanswered Questions*, p. 67.
17. John Macquarrie, *Thinking about God*. SCM Press 1975, pp. 56f. and 59.
18. Wessels, *Images of Jesus*, pp. 163–4. See also R. S. Sugirtharajah, ed., *Asian Faces of Jesus*. SCM Press 1993.

4

Responding Flexibly

It is one thing to tell the story of Charles Ives's childhood encounter with two bands converging on one another in Danbury Main Street. It is another, though, to show how that experience of two tunes heard simultaneously directly influenced his subsequent musical expression and composition. The most obvious thing to do is simply listen to a performance of his *Holidays Symphony* and hear how the 'two-tunes' experience is explicitly re-created in the movement depicting 'The Fourth of July'. However, there are also far more subtle and implicit examples of this experience permeating his large and varied output of symphonies, sonatas and songs. In many respects, Ives pre-empted the great mid-twentieth-century conflict between the protagonists of traditional tonal compositions and avant-garde atonal ones by the incorporation of both Schoenberg and Stravinsky into his own personality and creativity—many years before either of them began composing. His music is effectively a catalogue of worked examples illustrating the impact of that Danbury experience on the somewhat sterile and unimaginative musical environment in which he was nurtured and educated.

His was essentially a 'liberal' approach to musical expression in so far as it was open to new possibilities, committed to hearing and responding to the culture around him, pluralistic in its sources of inspiration, and honest in its claims. Indeed, one of Ives's most enigmatic works is entitled *The Unanswered Question*. In this short piece, a solo trumpet repeats a questioning phrase no less than seven times. Each time the phrase is answered by a wind band that takes the 'question' less and less seriously as it descends to a discordant ridiculing of the trumpet tune. Eventually, the 'question' is posed for the seventh and last time—and there is no answer. All we hear are the ethereal strings that have been providing a secure bass-line beneath the raucous interchange between the trumpeter and his colleagues in the band. There is something of eternity about these strings, suggesting that they were there before the questioning ever began, and they will still be there when all our more or less ridiculous answers will be shown up for what they are. It is an evocative piece capable of many interpretations. The 'question' may be about the future of religion, or music, or philosophy, but the message is that the answers always come off worst and the sustained ground-bass of unfathomable truth always has the last word.

We must now seek to provide examples of how a liberal approach to evangelism applies the 'two-tunes' experience to the vital business of making Christ knowable and known in our generation. We do so, though, in the spirit of Ives's *The Unanswered Question*, which allows the question to be heard long after all our answers have been tried—and the fundamental themes of faith, hope and love to be heard as a persistent reassurance and response to our insistent clamourings after truth. As we hear the tunes of tradition simultaneously with the melodies of modernity, we must be open and honest enough to acknowledge that the sum total of all our questions and answers will still fall short of plumbing the depths of God's being in the face of Christ, which will be for us, and for those to whom we minister, a means of grace and the hope of glory.

We propose to take a number of contemporary issues in ministry and mission and expose them to the approach decribed in the previous chapter. We shall seek to show how, in each case, a responsive and flexible methodology opens up evangelistic possibilities that are not realized when evangelism is more narrowly defined. The emphasis here is essentially on methodology, rather than a step-by-step guide to good practice! However, it is our hope that this approach will prove applicable to a wider range of contexts and situations than those singled out for particular attention here.

Caring to share

In the mid-1970s, a popular definition of Christian pastoral care ran as follows: 'helping acts, done by representative Christian

persons, directed towards the healing, sustaining, guiding and
reconciling of troubled persons whose troubles arise in the context of ultimate meanings and concerns'.[1] It will be observed that
there is little explicit reference here to any aspects of pastoral
care that might be termed specifically Christian. Most carers of
any religious persuasion, or none at all, could have assented to
this definition. It clearly avoids any hint of evangelistic intent
underlying and motivating pastoral activity on behalf of those in
need. To this extent, it might be seen as a definition very much
of its time and one influenced by the so-called 'secular' 1960s.

By the late 1980s, Stephen Pattison consciously adapts the
earlier definition in order to offer one of his own. For him,
Christian pastoral care 'is that activity, undertaken especially by
representative Christian persons, directed towards the elimination
and relief of sin and sorrow and the presentation of all people
perfect in Christ to God'.[2] Here we notice the use of traditional
Christian terminology, and even a biblical text, to suggest that
pastoral care is inextricably linked to the propagation of explicitly
Christian values and ideals. It articulates an evangelistic dimension such as would have been unthinkable among liberal writers
on pastoral care just a decade or so earlier. To that extent, it represents the bridging of a theological and ministerial gap between
pastoral care and evangelism that was characterized by a profound
mutual suspicion. Liberals of a 1960s vintage felt passionately
antagonistic towards any suggestion that acts of care might have
an evangelistic ulterior motive over and above the single imperative to care—and care again. This antagonism had been fuelled
by an anti-colonialism that condemned missionary activity in the
fields of medicine and education as means to an end, rather than
ends in themselves. Voluntary Service Overseas and the Peace
Corps offered idealistic young people the chance to take up John
Kennedy's torch that had been passed to their generation, and to
challenge oppression and deprivation, sorrow and pain, sustained
by the belief that 'all you need is love'. Somehow, care and
evangelism just didn't seem to mix.

On the other hand, definitions of evangelism in the 1960s and
1970s would rarely allude to pastoral care or social responsibility
as constituent parts of authentic evangelistic strategy. The
spectre of the 'social gospel' haunted the hearts and minds of
evangelical Christians to such an extent that it was difficult for

those socially minded among them to avoid taunts of betraying the true gospel in their pursuit of secular solutions. With the advent of the New Right in British and American politics, so the rhetoric turned to charges of politicizing the gospel instead of proclaiming it. However, the underlying message was the same: the currency of Christian evangelism must not be devalued by the base coinage of pastoral care and social work.

It was against this background that the Lambeth Conference of 1988, in calling for a Decade of Evangelism, passed Resolution 44 in the following words:

This conference:
1. Calls for a shift to a dynamic missionary emphasis going beyond care and nurture to proclamation and service; and therefore,
2. Accepts the challenge this presents to diocesan and local church structures and patterns of worship and ministry, and looks to God for fresh movement of the Spirit in prayer, outgoing love and evangelism in obedience to our Lord's Command.

Here we still see evidence of that divide of mutual suspicion between evangelism and pastoral care that has hindered the mission of the Church for much of the century. The bishops still see evangelism as something over and beyond pastoral care.

Yet we would want to argue that pastoral care is an essential part of the good news of God in Christ and evangelism cannot be truly evangelistic without a pastoral dimension. Furthermore, such pastoral care cannot be used merely as a means of bringing people within earshot of the gospel. A liberal approach to evangelism appeals to pastoral care as our way of coming within earshot of those in need. That is why SPCK's series entitled 'New Library of Pastoral Care' is more about the interdependence of carer and cared-for than the dependency relationship implied by most volumes in the original series. This interdependence is reflected in such titles as *Swift to Hear*[3] and *Being There*.[4] Pastoral care is not something we do to people, but something people do to, and for, each other in a mutuality of listening and responding. This is where the evangelistic quality of pastoral care emerges most strongly.

From all that we have said so far, it is clear that anything that involves listening before speaking or acting sits well with a liberal approach to evangelism. It is in day-to-day pastoral contact that we discover much of the grist for the evangelistic mill. Just as we cannot truly care in a valid and effective way unless we have listened and understood, so we cannot respond appropriately with good news of healing and salvation unless we have heard what 'the still, sad music of humanity' is saying to us about God and the gospel we have to proclaim. Then we might find ourselves able to draw on those tunes from Scripture and tradition that can bring harmony to discordant lives. Barbara and Tom Butler have put it very well: 'we can all participate in one another's mission by "being there", and through being there we help to open one another's eyes and hearts'.[5]

The parable of the sheep and the goats might be offered as the proof text for all this. After all, the parable is interpreted by Jesus so as to make it explicit that *he* was the hungry man, the homeless woman, the naked child, the helpless prisoner. In meeting with them we meet with him, so that our stock of faces of Christ is enriched by such encounters. At the same time, we draw on our store of 'faces' in order to find that face of Christ that meets that person as saviour and healer in their particular need. Effective pastoral care is when Jesus meets Jesus face to face, and there is good news—evangelism—in the encounter.

In recent years, Holocaust theology has familiarized us with 'the God of the Gallows', and Bishop John Robinson, in his deeply moving final sermon, has not been alone in identifying 'Christ in the cancer'. Thus we continue to be surprised by the God of surprises, who is to be found and known in the AIDS virus, Alzheimer's disease, the teenage suicide and the broken home. Listening for God and responding with Christ in ways appropriate and sensitive to the particularity of such human tragedies surely cannot be just a preamble to evangelism; instead, it is the very stuff of true evangelism and must be alongside all else that glories in the name.

In reflecting upon twenty or so years of pastoral ministry in search of examples to illustrate this section, I have found time and again that the experiences I have recalled have been remarkable for their lack of words. There was the young mother who had just learned of her husband's accidental death. As a new curate fresh from college and full of words, I felt there must be something I should say, but all I could do was hold her tight and weep with her and for her. Some weeks later, she told friends how that action by a tremulous and tongue-tied parson spoke more to her than all manner of comforting texts. Or then there was the middle-aged man in the depth of depression, to whom I spoke words he never heard, but who subsequently recalled how my hand holding his somehow felt like a lifeline in his dark despair. Such experiences simply reinforce the power of touch, about which Norman Autton[6] has written so eloquently, but they also give us a clue as to why evangelism has been so suspicious of pastoral care. For too many people, and for far too long, evangelism has been about the Word made wordy; but pastoral care is about the Word made flesh and dwelling among us. It is so often through the power of personal presence and human contact that the God in the suffering and the Christ in the pain are known afresh, and the healing power of God in Christ is transmitted at a level too deep for words.

Now it has to be said that there is nothing extraordinary or 'special' about all this. What is described here is being practised day by day by Christian people who are reluctant to call themselves evangelists. That, though, is precisely my point. Once this liberal approach to evangelism is acknowledged and affirmed, then it allows a tremendous range of people to 'own' the Decade of Evangelism, in ways not possible when definitions are drawn too narrowly. The fact of the matter is that a whole army of people in our churches are 'doing evangelism' as a normal and natural part of daily life, but they do not seem to feel themselves included in the prevailing evangelistic culture. If this is true, and they are 'doing' it, then we must hijack the slogan from the television DIY commercial and affirm that 'anything you can do, you can do better!' In our schemes of Christian education and training, let us acknowledge the listening and the caring and the 'being there' that are so much a part of people's lives, and build on them in such a way as to make clear our belief that caring is good news, and the good news is in the caring.

Human rites

This section follows on naturally upon the last because it is concerned with the occasional offices when the Church administers rites of baptism, marriage, burial or cremation.

What Wesley Carr calls *Brief Encounters*[7] are major points of contact between the Church and local communities. When clergy are about to leave a ministerial post, and look back at who has joined that worshipping community since his or her arrival, it will usually be the case that a significant number of them are there as a result of encounters at the time of childbirth, marriage or bereavement. Indeed, most ministers in small communities are only as good as their last funeral, and the quality of the ministry exercised on such occasions can make or break an incumbency.

These are occasions when flexibility, sensitivity and responsiveness are at a premium. Of course, it is possible to get away with simply reading the set service whatever the individual circumstances of those involved, but the result of so doing invariably amounts to a pastoral disaster. These are occasions when individuals need to be publicly named and their individuality ritually affirmed and celebrated. On occasions, I have arrived at the crematorium in time to hear the service preceding the one at which I will be officiating. It is instructive to note down as much as I can about the deceased person and their circumstances on the basis of what is said during the service I am overhearing. Sadly, there have been times when my notes add up to no more than a name—and, on one or two occasions, not even as much as that. Such failure to personalize the rite is not only to commit a major psychological mistake, it is also to miss an important evangelistic opportunity.

It is never appropriate to use the occasional offices as blatantly evangelistic events, because this will almost certainly subvert the primary function of the service as a crucial stage in the process of transition from one status to another—single to married, married to widowed, and so on. However, the kind of liberal evangelism described in this book is entirely suited to such occasions. Indeed, this is precisely what good ministers are about when they take the trouble to prepare for such services, and to conduct them with care and attention to detail.

First of all, there will be time spent with the parents, the couple, or the mourners, observing and listening in order to personalize the rite and contextualize it as sensitively as possible. It is during these times spent together that the minister begins to sense the point these people have reached in their emotional, intellectual and spiritual development, and through the stories they tell he will glimpse something of the journeys they have made towards and away from God in the course of their lives. Next there comes a time of reflection on what has been felt and heard. At the same time, resources of Scripture and tradition are plundered for that face of Christ, that word of salvation that will be responsive to those people at that moment in their lives. It is these threads woven into the loose fabric of the rite that can make the occasion as unique as the person or persons it seeks to serve. Put another way, what those involved will be pleased to call 'our tune' is heard simultaneously with the tunes of tradition, and the effectiveness of the rite will be directly related to this dynamic of social, psychological and religious integration.

These are occasions when we are called not so much to speak with people or to people, as to speak for them. We are often being asked to say what is felt too deep for words, and thus to say what people find so difficult to say for themselves. This is true even when we have had very little opportunity to visit them or to get to know them—as is the case with the 'rota' funeral at the crematorium. Even then it is possible to provide a suggestive framework by means of which the participants can hear said what they want to say. On many occasions, people have told me that I have spoken of someone as if I had known them all my life, when in reality my knowledge was extremely sketchy. This was not because I took a risk and simply guessed at the truth—this is never acceptable. Rather, it was because I had simply spoken in such a way, and conducted the service in such a manner, as to ensure that enough gaps were left between the words and actions for those present to fill them with their own thoughts, feelings and memories. In subsequent sections we will be arguing that such 'meaning-gaps' are vital in effective worship and Bible study in most situations, but it is especially so when we are seeking to respond wisely and well to the needs of those whose rites of passage we are privileged to share.

It is when people feel that their story has been heard, their heartfelt feelings articulated, and their hopes and fears addressed, that they come away with a sense of having been encountered by something or someone beyond themselves at a vital stage in their journey. Of course, much will be projected on to the minister, and it has to be said that sometimes the sense of encounter never sees beyond the minister to the God he or she is there to represent. Sometimes, though, the rites relating to birth, marriage and death are critical turning points in terms of how people relate to the gospel, and this is most likely to be the case when the ministry has been open, honest, adaptable and genuinely responsive to how and where people actually are.

Because the strategy of flexible response is such a natural way of ministering at the occasional offices, it is clear that liberal evangelists will want to make themselves and their congregations as available as possible for such purposes. They will probably have little truck with hard-line baptism policies or preconditions for marriage or funerals in church. They will welcome the opportunities provided for them by the general assumption that churches are user-friendly for these purposes, even with regard to otherwise unchurched members of the community. They will rejoice that, for once, people are seeking them out for a ministry so that responsiveness is a given element in the relationship—which is not often the case when church people find themselves taking the initiative. By no means least, they are aware of the fact that it is very often those who are not members of the immediate family or circle of close friends who feel touched by the ministry exercised at baptisms, weddings and funerals. The ripples of responsiveness reach beyond those most intimately involved and touch the troubled marriage in the fourth row at the wedding, or the frightened cancer sufferer in the back pew at the crematorium. Once again, we discover that caring is good news, and this good news can be shared in even the briefest of brief encounters.

Taking stock

In recent years we have seen a steady growth in proposals and schemes for 'taking stock' of communities and situations as the precondition for programmes of pastoral care and/or evangelistic activity. By and large, this development is to be welcomed. Here is a clear acknowledgement that the effective sharing of the Christian message cannot happen without an informed awareness of the prevailing culture and context. Sometimes this is known as pre-evangelism, and we can detect obvious parallels with the growth in market-research techniques employed by manufacturers and retailers. Indeed, many of those promoting this kind of approach as a prelude to missionary activity grew up under the influence of Vance Packard's *The Hidden Persuaders*.[8] This book set out to horrify us with grisly accounts of subliminal advertising techniques, but also seduced us with its promise of effective results in proportion to efficient research into the market.

While those concerned with Faith in the City and Countryside have promoted the importance of 'taking stock' as a vital first step in our appreciation and renewal of local communities, John Finney is foremost among those who have harnessed this requirement to the task of contemporary evangelism. Like Wagner's music, Finney's *The Well-church Book*[9] is better than it sounds! He puts major emphasis on getting to know the community within which any church is set, and he adapts the pastoral cycle sequence of Experience–Interpretation–Reflection–Action in order to demonstrate how looking and listening must precede proclamation. As Philip King has written: 'It is helpful to remember that the word "audit" has the idea of listening—we need to listen to the hopes and needs of the community around.'[10]

However, like most types of pre-evangelism techniques, the aim in Finney's approach is both to soften up the local community with assurances of concern for their well-being, and to listen out for signals indicating the kinds of linguistic and conceptual packaging most appropriate to this particular context. As Finney himself argues at the conclusion of his own research entitled *Finding Faith Today*:

> Evangelization needs to be founded upon fact rather than fantasy. Many industrial companies spend 15–20% of their turnover on research and development. The Churches in this country have a turnover of many millions and yet I doubt if the amount spent on research is as much as half of one per cent. As a result money is wasted, the time of Christians is squandered, and most important of all, people do not hear the good news of God in Christ in a way they can respond to.[11]

As we have suggested earlier, this is all very well as far as it goes, but there is little to suggest that the process of 'market research' will actually affect the content of the message in addition to controlling the manner of its delivery. However, we

Liberal Evangelism

would want to argue that a liberal approach to evangelism is flexible not only in its responding with an appropriate vocabulary, but in its readiness to discover new insights with respect to the content of the gospel itself. Furthermore, it will be flexible in its responding with a face of Christ and a promise of salvation specific to what has been seen and heard.

So when we undertake our audits, with our visitations, street interviews, questionnaires and statistical surveys, can we also be alert to what all this may have to tell us about the kind of God we believe in and the kind of gospel we are called to proclaim? Grace Davie tells of how a woman was stopped in the street and asked if she believed in God. She said that she did. She was then asked if she believed in the God who made the world and who sent Jesus to be our Saviour. 'No,' she said, 'just the ordinary one.' Who is this 'ordinary' God she said she believed in? Have we something to learn from her about God's ordinariness—and to what extent is the face of Jesus an ordinary face looking upon all ordinary people and things, events and eventualities, and making them special through his gaze? Some might say that the sacramentalization of the ordinary is at the heart of sacramental theology, yet how often we have allowed the specialness of sacraments to obscure the presence of an 'ordinary' God seeking to save us through the very ordinariness of himself in the Man from Nazareth.

Likewise, encounters with whole communities can be revelations in themselves—even before we have begun to reveal the good news we are there to share. This was the case with one small market town surveyed as part of a mission audit and appraisal programme. The fine medieval church stood proud and noble in the centre of the town square. This church had strong civic links, and a large proportion of the population found themselves within its walls for special services, occasional offices and regular concerts. It was a hub of activity and a testimony to the continued significance and vitality of the Christian religion in a small town in England. Yet the majority of parishioners had no sense at all of that significance or vitality. They had no purchase on that frenetic round of liturgical spectaculars and festivals of music and drama—let alone the daily and weekly round of prayer and worship. In spite of appearances, the church community had wrapped itself around with a tight-fitting garment that left little by way of a hem to trail out into the wider community. It was only when they heeded the results of their survey, and acknowledged that their God was a God working at the fringes and not only at the centre of things, that they began to loosen that close-fitting garment and allow a hem to trail into the community to be touched by those as yet untouched by the gospel. This they did through the use of their splendid new hall for community groups that ranged from mother-and-toddler groups to a senior-citizens' day centre. There is nothing especially new or original about any of this, but it arose out of a new awareness of God met in the marginalized and revealed in the face of the Jesus who allowed power to go out through the hem of his garment, and who called into his healing presence a woman weakened by years of haemorrhaging and outcast from respectable society. Her successors found a hem to touch in that market town, and experienced something of that healing power of Christ whose face they could never have recognized behind the inscrutable mask of civic religion.

This is but one example of how a readiness to take stock of the community around us, to listen creatively to its sighs and celebrations, and to know its needs and aspirations at first hand, reveals God to us in new and unexpected ways. Mention could also have been made of the middle-aged mother of four on a grim post-war housing estate, who came to a church-based adult literacy group after the priest discovered in his survey of the parish that inability to read was a major barrier to church attendance. For her, the word literally became flesh in the face of a somewhat severe but deeply compassionate solicitor's wife, who painstakingly helped her to read and write. Or what about the church set in the wealthiest suburb of a large commercial city that discovered via a survey that the community was characterized by a large proportion of wealthy widows and lonely au pairs! This church set up an advice service staffed by accountants in the congregation to meet the anxieties of those unused to managing money, and a support group for those girls vulnerable and isolated in a foreign country. Biblical injunctions to care for the widows and the aliens in our midst took a somewhat surprising turn in this case, but surely there is a God to be met in the widow's wealth as well as the widow's mite—and our scriptural tradition offers for us to share the face of a Christ concerned

both for the rich and the poor, the lonely Swedish teenager as
well as the rootless refugee.

These are ways in which a flexible response to the findings of
mission audit can ensure that our evangelism is specific to the
needs of our culture and context. However, it also ensures openness to truth, wherever it may be found and wherever it may lead.
It is committed to listening before speaking and acting. It celebrates the rich variety of the gospel and is honest in its expecta-
tions that what we proclaim must always provide for the insights
and inspirations of those to whom we proclaim it.

Liturgical response

Why do we worship the way we do? Answers to this question
are many and varied, with repeated appeals to the precedent of
the early Church, medieval practice, reformed principles or contemporary vernacular needs. In recent decades the liturgical
movement has placed a high premium on being in tune with the
first Christian believers when it comes to the drafting of alternative liturgies. In *The Shape of the Liturgy*,[12] Dom Gregory Dix
beguiled a whole generation with the promise of a pattern for
eucharistic worship that would put us firmly in a direct liturgical
line reaching back to at least third-century Rome and possibly to
New Testament times. Much of this assurance has been under-
mined by recent research, which points to a degree of pluralism
in early church worship unacknowledged by most liturgiologists
this century (see especially Paul Bradshaw, *The Search for the
Origins of Christian Worship*[13]). Yet the prevalence of liturgical
fundamentalism, rooted in Hippolytus, Calvin, Cranmer or the
Council of Trent, persists unabated in mainstream Churches.
How much energy must have been expended in arguments for
and against even the most modest liturgical reform! On the one
hand, keeping things as they are (with the implication that this is
how they always have been) is pitched against claims for
relevance, and up-to-date liturgy 'in the present tense'. The result
has often proved unsatisfactory to either side of the argument.
For example, the Alternative Service Book hardly satisfies those
who value the mantra-like mystique of fundamentalist texts—
usually represented by the Book of Common Prayer. Neither,
though, does it carry conviction with those looking for liturgies

in the vernacular of today's kitchens, classrooms, offices and dole queues.

The fault almost certainly lies in the quest for that elusive holy grail called Common Prayer. A recent General Synod debate proved remarkable for the passion with which this notion was affirmed and defended. All the proposer of the motion wanted was a little more freedom to experiment with orders for family worship and one-off liturgies for special occasions. What he stirred up was a deep-seated commitment to forms of words and patterns of ritual consistently rehearsed across all manner of historical, social and cultural divides. Knowing and understanding what we are all doing seemed to come second in importance to the need for us all to be doing it. Scholarship purporting to demonstrate that the much-loved texts and practices are in any sense critically suspect will carry as little weight with liturgical fundamentalists as the findings of critical scholarship have been found to carry with biblical fundamentalists. The tunes of tradition must be heard in our churches, even if the ears to hear them become fewer and fewer and the capacity to hear them diminishes year by year.[14]

Yet the claims of evangelism are now too pressing for us to absolve liturgy and worship from the need to make a clear contribution to the task of winning people for Christ. Worship is not something to which people are introduced *after* they have been introduced to the gospel. Worship is a primary tool of evangelism, and if we are going to break out of the sterile cycle of confrontation between the traditionalists and the trendies, then something like the liberal approach to evangelism that we are advocating will need to be given a hearing. For surely it is the case that when the tunes of tradition are heard simultaneously with the melodies of modernity in the context of corporate worship, lives have been changed and conversions have been commonplace.

The essential principles apply as much here as they do to pastoral care. We are required to listen hard to the wider community within which the worshipping community is set, and we are committed to discovering within our store of liturgical treasures that face of Christ that will comfort, challenge and change that community according to its need. This was the conclusion reached by the authors of *Faith in the City*:

Worship in the Urban Priority Areas must emerge out of and reflect local cultures: it will always be the worship of Him who is totally other and yet is to be found, worshipped and served through the realities of UPA life. . . . It will be more informal and flexible in its use of urban languge, vocabulary, style and content. It will therefore reflect a universality of form with local variations, allowing significant space for worship which is genuinely local, expressed in and through local cultures, and reflecting the local context.[15]

Here is a plea for us to bring together 'Him who is totally other' and that 'which is genuinely local'; to integrate with 'universality of form' that which is 'informal and flexible'. And why? Because 'the worship of the local church is important as a means of evangelism'.[16] The Liturgical Commission produced *Patterns for Worship*[17] as a response to this plea, and it remains to be seen just how successful it has been. At least, though, it is now clearly on the Church's agenda that worship is a function of evangelism, and truly evangelistic worship must be open, honest, flexible and responsive with respect to the prevailing culture.

To be fair, Catholic Christendom has always seen the liturgy as a tool of mission, with its strong emphasis on Christ made present, received and then served in the life of the world. It has to be acknowledged, though, that the mission of the Mass as a means of evangelism in local contexts has not always been in evidence, notwithstanding the Vatican II reforms and the modern inculturation movement. There needs to be a much stronger emphasis on the context as the provider not only of media and metaphors for worship, but of meaning as well. We have assumed that the meaning of worship is part of the givenness of it all, which has then to be translated and transmitted in acceptable ways—or simply handed down in traditional ways to be taken or left as the case may be. The meaning of worship, though, is not in the texts or the rituals. The meaning is in the minds and memories and experiences of communities and individuals offered up in penitence, prayer and praise and reflected back in that face of Christ encountering them in the uniqueness of their here and now. So this might mean that there will be as many understandings of what is going on in an act of worship as there are people participating. That *should* be the case if our worship is open, honest, flexible and responsive; and we will rejoice that this is the case when we affirm that the rich store of liturgical tradition is not the source of meaning for worship, but a resource for responding appropriately and creatively with meanings that challenge and change people into the likeness of Christ. Surely this is at least part of what evangelism is all about.

What will this mean for worship in local churches? First and foremost, it will mean a readiness to shift from liturgies in search of a context to contexts in search of liturgies. Most clergy have been trained to be extremely familiar with the history and content of prescribed liturgical texts and to apply them more or less appropriately to the prevailing context. We are wanting to suggest that the really important task is to know well the given context and to structure liturgical events responsive to that reality. Secondly, it will mean that liturgical texts must be treated as resources—servants and not masters. They are there to be used, and nowadays they are there in some profusion. Because a Church like the Church of England articulates its distinctive doctrinal stance through liturgy rather than formulae, there will always be need for controls on permitted texts. However, there remains plenty of scope to enact those texts in ways that enable people to find their own meaning taking shape in the spaces between the words and actions. Thirdly, it will mean that local worship will not only say things the way local people want to say them, but will say the things local people want to say. This will require commitment to the real presence of the Church in the community hearing, registering and representing the images of humanity struggling to find itself reflected in the image of God. In so far as we are talking about Sunday worship, all that we do then must be shot through with the stuff of Monday to Saturday—a pit stop for repairs and refuelling for a few more laps rather than a bolt hole to which escape can be made from the rigours of reality. By no means least, though, it means that worship will be open to a God who surprises creation by taking even the tiredest of old texts and through them making all things new—or, conversely, the trendiest of new texts to tell the old, old story. Something happens in worship when there is an air of expectancy, but what happens is seldom what we expect. That is why worship has an important place in a liberal approach to evangelism. It provides opportunities to be responsive in relation to the *world*, and creative in relation to the *word*. Let us seek in our meetings for worship to create an environment in which the resources of tradition are brought face to face with the realities of today—and the good news of God is there at the place of meeting.

A word for all seasons

The popular television game show *Blankety-Blank* required a studio audience to suggest words that might appropriately fill the blank left in a simple sentence. Contestants then guessed which of the suggestions was likely to have been most popular with the audience. Biblical 'blankety-blank' is a good game for getting a Bible study session off the ground. The text to target is Luke 2.49—and particularly the Greek phrase 'en tois tou patros mou', which translates literally as 'in the —— of my father'. The plural of the definite article is used instead of a specific noun. Raymond E. Brown[18] explores three possible ways of filling the blank. First of all, using the Authorized Version, we could translate 'Wist ye not that I must be *about my Father's business*'. Secondly, we could opt for the Revised Standard Version/New English Bible: 'Did you not know that I must be *in my Father's house*'. Thirdly, there is the less familiar Patristic version: 'Did you not know that I must be *in the household* [i.e. among the people] *of my Father*'. The fact of the matter is that any of these translations is feasible and the preferred version may well depend on the prejudices and assumptions of the reader. For example, I tried this out on a typical Sunday morning congregation and, just like the television *Blankety-Blank* format, I asked them to vote for the one they thought most likely to be correct. The vast majority divided evenly between 'business' and 'household', while only the two churchwardens opted for 'house'! For this group of Christians, thoughts of the building as the primary locus of divine activity trailed far behind their prejudice towards seeing the Kingdom of God in terms of 'people' and 'activity'. We know that other groups in different places or at various points in history would vote otherwise. Here is a clear example of how textual ambiguity allows even the least tutored of readers to have a go at biblical translation. There is, quite literally, a gap that must be filled if the text is to acquire a meaning, and that meaning is supplied by the reader filling the gap according to their own interpretative assumptions. And there are many modern biblical commentators who would argue that such 'blanks' are there to be filled in every biblical text because the reader is the essential purveyor of meaning.

Reader-response criticism has emerged as an approach to the biblical text that is concerned less with the intention of the author than with the reader's creation of meaning for himself or herself. Margaret Davies has written of this approach as follows:

> Reading is a co-operative endeavour. Through its literary conventions and strategies, the text presents a puzzle, which the reader must solve to aid understanding. The reader is drawn into the adventure not only by what the text spells out but also by what it withholds. To understand literature, the reader must begin to fill in the gaps, to infer what is not given, at least provisionally, until what is unclear at first is clarified by what follows.[19]

In terms of the history of biblical criticism, it is fair to say that there has been a significant shift in recent years away from the search for 'what really happened' and the quest for clarity as to what the original authors 'really meant'. The spotlight has been turned from the event and the author who described the event towards the text bequeathed to us by the author (whoever that might have been) in describing the event (whatever it was that actually occurred). In one sense, this can be used to get us off the hook of historical and source criticism by focusing exclusively on the givenness of the text. Indeed, the attractiveness of this approach is clear to those seeking to affirm scriptural authority in the teeth of critical techniques perfected over the last two hundred years. It is argued that the true miracle of revelation is located in the givenness of the canon of Scripture rather than in the historicity of any particular events or persons recounting those events. Of course, this transference of authority to the givenness of the text raises enormous problems of its own. After all, the determination of the canon was itself an historical process activated by very human beings. Historico-critical methods can be applied as much to this process as to the processes involved in the composition of the constituted books forming the final canon—in so far as it is possible to speak of a final canon when agreement as to its contents has been far from unanimous!

Thus this turning to the text can be hijacked by postmodernists seeking a return to pre-Enlightenment certainties, after the discomfiture caused by critical and clinical dissection of Holy Scripture and long-trusted tradition. However, a more appropriate approach—and, as it happens, a more appropriately liberal approach to this focusing on the text—is available to us. Basically, it can be argued that the text is not there to be taken as read, but there to be taken *and* read. It is in the reader's response to the text that the 'truth' of the text is to be identified and valued. At a minimum, this may be saying no more than that the authors meant more than they realized. The reader then responds with meanings that supplement the author's meaning. Thus the sequence of event–author–text needs to be completed by the reader's response to the text. Thoroughgoing deconstructionalists will go farther by discounting the significance of the preliminary event–author stages so as to establish the locus of meaning in the reading, and not in the writing, of the text. Accordingly, readers are invited to read themselves into the text without any illusions of 'the original meaning'.[20]

By way of example, we can take the infancy narrative of Matthew. If we simply concentrate on the author's intention with respect to the text, then the message is obvious. The birth of Jesus is told with obvious reference to the birth of Moses. Jesus is being compared with the great hero of the Hebrew scriptures with the clear implication that here is One who is even greater. The author's meaning is fundamentally Christological in its intention. If we take the line that the author meant more than he realized, then the reader is entitled to read beyond the elevation of Jesus above Moses to the conclusion that here is One who is greater than *anyone* who went before him. The fact that Luke pursues the same 'you ain't seen nothin' yet' approach, but in his case using John the Baptist as the comparitor, adds weight to the reader's broader conclusions. Here the reader goes beyond Matthew's Christological intention towards a more eschatological meaning—Jesus fulfils and transcends all that has gone before, thus signalling the in-breaking of God's Kingdom in a new and decisive mission. If we go further, and argue that there is a 'meaning-gap' to be filled by the reader, and the reader alone, then it is the superior greatness of Jesus in relation to the reader's own prior values and assumptions that will decide what the text signifies. The reading may then turn out to be more socio-political than Christological or eschatological. Jesus is greater than any in my personal hall of heroes, and so I enlist him in support of my causes and concerns. Thus Matthew's infancy narrative becomes a political or liberationist or feminist text as the case may be.

Put this way, the dangers in reader-response criticism are very obvious. After all, what is there to prevent the reader simply finding in the text what he or she wants to find? There is a real risk that just as 'theology' has become a synonym for ideological dogmatism, so Bible study is likewise reduced to ideology. In an attempt to escape from the tyranny of authorial intention, we find ourselves submitting to the interpretative dicta of the reader's personal agenda.

The only way to avoid both of these fates, while still affirming the liberating value of reader-response, is to insist that the text is the locus of meaning for both the author *and* the reader. It is reasonable to ask, 'What did the author mean?', but it is equally reasonable to ask, 'What does it mean to me?' True profit, though, lies in asking these questions simultaneously. Matthew's meaning and my meaning need each other if we are to avoid the irrelevancies of historical particularism on the one hand, and the arrogance of ideological appropriation on the other. If the author's intention is all that matters in Bible study, then the text is consigned to the deep-freeze of literary history. If the meaning given to the text by the reader is all that matters, then Humpty Dumpty is the patron saint of hermeneutics!

Here we are again with something like the two-tunes experience that is at the heart of a liberal approach to evangelism. Creative Bible study involves hearing the author's intentions simultaneously with the reader's response, so that a truly meaningful tune is heard over and above ancient and modern claims for exclusive rights to the *real* meaning of it all. That is why Bible study has an important part to play in a liberal evangelistic strategy.

It is not simply a matter of participation. There has been no shortage of guides to participatory Bible study in recent years and these are to be welcomed. Hans Reudi Weber has conducted brilliant *Experiments with Bible Study*[21] involving thousands of participants on any one occasion, and the Ignatian approach to Gospel meditation invites people to enter the scene by imagination and identify with characters in the story.[22] Such personal engagement with the text can be profoundly disturbing and life-changing in its implications; but we want to go on to suggest the evangelistic importance not only of the reader becoming identified with Blind Bartimaeus, but of Blind Bartimaeus becoming identified with the reader. I respond effectively to this story when he is me and his blindness is mine and his new-found sight is new-found sight for me also. This happens when the reader is encouraged to own his or her sense of blindness in such a way as to ensure that the author's meaning becomes focused in that moment of encounter with the text and so transfigures the reality of the reader's experience to the point where once-darkened eyes are ablaze with a new vision. Indeed, in such a case it may be said that the reader does not so much respond to the text, as the text responds to the reader—thus affirming the truth of the old adage that I do not read the Bible, but the Bible reads me! However, it is not one thing *or* the other. It is both at the same time. The reader comes to the text equipped with values, prejudices and meanings, and in the study of the text—alone or with others—encounters a meaning intended for the text by the author, and both are changed as the meaning-gap is filled by a transfiguring truth. Walter Wink has written about *Transforming Bible Study*,[23] and it is nothing less that we are claiming for that moment when author and reader meet around a text and lives are changed.

A liberal Christian is likely to have difficulties with ancient texts that impose their meaning on modern readers. A liberal Christian will also have difficulty with that kind of radicalism that imposes modern meanings on to ancient texts. However, a liberal Christian should be active in any approach to the biblical text that is honest in its acceptance of biblical criticism, open to the importance of authorial intention *and* reader response, flexible in its celebration of many meanings, and committed to the responsiveness of the text to meeting the meanings and the needs of those who engage with it. Bible study that fulfils these criteria will be effectively liberal in its theological provenance and genuinely evangelistic in its purpose and goal.

Many faiths—one God

So far we have been concentrating on the implications of a liberal approach to evangelism for such general areas of church life as pastoral care, mission audit, worship and Bible study. However, we must also demonstrate the specific relevance of this approach for our engagement with people professing a faith different from our own. In the past, this has mainly taken place overseas and in unfamiliar cultural contexts. All that has been said so far about opening our ears to prevailing cultural norms and conventions, and responding appropriately with the resources our Christian tradition puts at our disposal, applies with equal force when the mission encounter is on foreign soil. Indeed, we have already examined Vincent Donovan's life work among the Masai in the light of our proposed strategy. Such encounters, though, are now a major element in the life of Christians here in Britain, who are increasingly likely to find themselves living, working and worshipping in multi-faith communities. Consequently, inter-faith relationships and the appropriateness of mainstream evangelistic activity in multi-faith situations has crept towards the top of the agenda in most of our churches. A number of key theological issues are focused in debates on this topic and we want to demonstrate that a flexible response strategy has an important contribution to make to such debates.

Barbara and Tom Butler have provided us with a helpful lead into this discussion:

> Our own experience is that if we enter into encounter and dialogue with people of other faiths we may realise that God is there, and that his love is shown both in the people of other faiths and in the encounter itself. It is often sad to realise that many Christians who oppose inter-faith encounter and dialogue have no experience of it and may be looking in the wrong direction, towards themselves, and asking the wrong questions, namely 'How does this affect us and how do we defend our faith?', rather than expecting faith to be strengthened and expanded. True, it is not possible fully to appreciate

a faith, including Christianity, without entering it, and thereby having the 'eye of faith'. Christians may however look away from themselves and may then see what God is doing through the people of other faiths, and through this learn more about and respect the spiritual journey of their neighbour. Indeed this encounter with those of other faiths can be a 'mirror' which teaches us more about our own spiritual journey by illuminating and deepening our approach to God through Jesus Christ in the power of the Holy Spirit.[24]

The point has been made even more powerfully by John Taylor, and in terms that resonate clearly with our own:

> Those who have the habit of thinking about their own convictions and who view their understanding of God as a continuous discovery are able not only to recognize common ground in the things to which they and the followers of another faith bear witness, but also to discern the different faces attributed in the different faiths to the concept we call 'God', and the different values and hopes that are derived from those different faces. Hinduism has borne her patient testimony to the inclusive Oneness of God, Islam has passionately proclaimed his Sovereignty, Judaism his moral Faithfulness. 'Such differences', says a Christian thinker after six years of study in the holy city of Varanasi, 'have often led, tragically, to arid disputes, fanatisicm, and mutual anathema. The remedy for this is not to abandon our convictions, as is fashionable in some Western Christian quarters today, but to expose them to the full force of what the other man says. This can lead us to make new discoveries about our own faith.' Such self-discovery, clarifying the particular understanding of God to which one's own religion bears its most characteristic witness, is the task to which the pluralism of our day impels us. The different 'faces' of God which are set forth will seem in some respects to be mutually contradictory, and for a long time we may not be ready to guess how, if at all, they will be reconciled. I believe we can confidently leave that in the hands of the future if we will only persevere in the agenda for today.[25]

We cannot ignore what is being said here about our own faith being illuminated by encounter with people of other faiths. So many of those much-loved mission hymns dwell on the illuminating power of the gospel. We assert how 'O'er heathen lands afar, thick darkness broodeth yet' and triumphantly proclaim 'and in earth's darkest place, Let there be Light!' Little acknowledgement is made that light from other faiths may illuminate the darker recesses of our own faith and so help facets of our faith to shine in new and exciting ways.

It is now commonplace to classify theological approaches to other faiths under three headings: exclusivism, inclusivism and pluralism.[26] Broadly speaking, this offers us the choice between other faiths as wrong, true up to a point, and true! Evangelistically, the respective strategies amount to proclamation, negotiation and abdication! We will not go into each of these models here because that has been well covered elsewhere, and because we agree with David Bosch's belief that 'we are in need of a theology of religions characterised by creative tension, which reaches beyond the sterile alternative between a comfortable claim to absoluteness and arbitrary pluralism'.[27] Somehow, the 'true up to a point' approach does not meet this requirement, perhaps because Karl Rahner's description of those of other faiths as 'anonymous Christians' is altogether too patronizing for modern ears. Also, the implication that other faiths are only fulfilled when they find their fulfilment in Christ seems only different in degree, and not in kind, from the triumphalist claims of exclusivism. Though much favoured by liberals in the past, this idea that in relation to other religions Christianity is still the best, and is sure to outlive them, is not popular today.

Most modern liberals would look with favour on the pluralistic approach. After all, this seems to give appropriate weight to that openness that is a crucial aspect of liberalism. The writings of John Hick on this subject have struck chords with many as he expounds the God of many names. Likewise, Keith Ward has offered *A Vision to Pursue*[28] that readily finds favour with those anxious to minimize the often bloody consequences of inter-faith rivalry and to affirm the unique contribution that each tradition can make to convergent and emerging world-wide truths and values.

However, as Bosch puts it, all three models are found wanting because 'they are all too neat'. He goes on:

> They all work out too well. In the end everything—and every-
> one!—is accounted for. There are no loose ends, no room left
> for surprises and unsolved puzzles. . . . The various models
> seem to leave no room for embracing the abiding paradox of
> asserting both ultimate commitment to one's own religion and
> genuine openness to another's.[29]

This is precisely what the 'two-tunes' approach seeks to achieve.
No one is being asked to demonstrate their commitment to one
tune by simply playing it louder in order to drown out the other.
Neither is anyone being asked to suppress their own tune in
misguided deference to the other. Rather, the claims of
Christianity are heard simultaneously with those of other faiths
and, in so far as there is dissonance, it could be that it is only
'dissonant voices' that really speak the truth.[30]

For example, 'two-covenant theology' has emerged as a dom-
inant influence on Jewish–Christian relations since the Second
World War. It argues that the covenant between Yahweh and
Israel still stands because God is faithful and does not renegue
on promises. The good news of God in Christ is not a new covenant
in the sense of replacing what had gone before, but another
covenant reaching beyond the Jewish people to embrace all nations.
'The issue for the early Church concerned the inclusion of the
Gentiles in God's saving work, not the exclusion of the Jews'.[31]

This means that what we call the 'Old' Testament is still as
fresh as new paint to the Jews, and it remains full of relevance
and immediacy as a record of God's dealings with humanity and
all creation. It then becomes distinctly questionable whether the
conversion of Jews to Christianity in terms of their abandoning
one faith for the sake of another makes any real sense. Surely
evangelism with respect to Judaism must be seen more in terms
of mutuality. Both the 'old' and 'new' covenants are abiding
covenants coexisting as different but complementary insights
into the purposes of God. We must reject 'supercessionism',
which asserts that members of the Christian Church have simply
replaced Jews as the People of God. The Lambeth bishops put it
very well: 'We firmly reject any view of Judaism which sees it
as a living fossil, simply superseded by Christianity.'[32]

Here, two covenantal tunes are being played at the same time
and we need to hear both. This is not in order to appreciate how

one fulfils the other, or to show how one says the same as the other—both these approaches, and others, are to be found in our lectionaries—but in order to enrich our awareness of God's unrelenting zeal to save and sanctify people and peoples by whatever means may achieve that end. We encounter the adherents of Judaism as people who have much to learn and much to share. Evangelistically, what we share of the Christian covenant will clearly reflect what we have learned from the covenant with the people of Israel, and the two tunes will together reveal more of the truth than either can contain alone.[33]

Now it is usual among those who espouse two-covenant theology to argue for the Jews being, in this respect, a special case. As Schalom ben Chorin has put it: 'the faith *of* Jesus unites us; faith *in* Jesus divides us'. Our common roots make it inappropriate to treat Jews in the same way as others who do not acknowledge Christ. However, our common roots also make it inappropriate to extend the indulgence to those outside the Judaeo-Christian tradition. Yet there are good grounds for challenging this position.

Andre Karamaga is a Rwandan theologian and, taking his title from the nickname for that small and beautiful mountainous country, he published in 1988 *Dieu au pays des mille collines* and subtitled it *Quand l'Afrique recontre l'Evangile*. In the course of expounding the nature of this encounter between Africa and the gospel, he explores the question: 'Have the Rwandans their own Old Testament?' He answers by showing how the Hebrew Scriptures show people facing the same trials and sharing the same experiences as the Rwandan people, and thus concludes that the Old Testament is for them because it tells of them just as it tells of the Jewish people in their wanderings, exodus, exile and resettlement in the land.

Yet it could be argued the other way round. Why should Karamaga not conclude that because the Old Testament accurately reflects the history of the Rwandans' struggle to find truth and meaning, so their story is just as much *the* 'Old Testament' for them as the Law and Prophets are for Judaism? Has not God been searching for them through the religious beliefs and practices—however 'primitive'—that have characterized their history? What 'covenants' might he have struck with them, and with other peoples, in distant times and far-off places? Maybe there is a sense in which 'other faiths' are in fact other 'covenants' needing

to be heard simultaneously with the covenantal good news of
God in Christ, so that, as the Butlers put it, we can 'expect to
find that our own Christian faith is deepened and enriched by
viewing it from a different perspective'.[34]

The basis for this understanding of other faiths as other
covenants is to be found in the concept of a universal covenant
expounded in the opening chapters of Genesis and maintained
throughout Hebrew and Christian Scriptures. While it is true that
our 'old' and 'new' Testaments concentrate on God's specific
covenants with his people—both the people of Israel and those
who are 'in Christ'—there is no denying God's primary covenantal
relationship with all creation and all creatures. As Wesley
Ariarajah has expressed it:

> It is indeed significant that the Bible begins with the affirma-
> tion of the common humanity of all people, both in their
> participation in the life of God (image) and in their state of
> alienation from that source of life (the 'fall'). . . . It is surely
> not without interest that the opening chapters choose to speak
> of the human family as a whole rather than deal with a section
> of it.[35]

He goes on to show how the universal covenant that God makes
with Noah in fact goes beyond humanity to embrace all living
things:

> The special word 'covenant', which implies mutual trust and
> responsibility, is used to describe the relationship between
> God and all of creation. . . . The biblical story could easily
> have begun with chapter 12 with the call of Abraham. But
> there seems to be almost a conscious attempt to place the
> story of Israel in the broader context of God's creative,
> redemptive and covenant relationship with the whole of
> humanity and all created order.

Furthermore, the very strong biblical theme of special election
by God of a 'chosen people' has to be seen within the context of
a modest but recurring emphasis on God as the Lord of all
nations. The most famous reference is to the Persian king Cyrus
(Isaiah 45.1), but this is but one example of how the Bible
recounts and celebrates the universal Lordship of God over all

peoples and nations. Having examined a range of such references, Ariarajah concludes:

> . . . all yearnings for God, all attempts to know and love God, however right or wrong, appropriate or inappropriate, happen within God's providence. A radical recovery of God as creator means that my Hindu or Buddhist neighbour, whether I like or dislike the way he or she worships God, is still the child of God. God is as much his or her creator as mine. For there is no other God but the God who is the source of all being. . . . It is this biblical faith that drives us into dialogue. If my Hindu, Buddhist, or Muslim neighbour is as much a child of God as I am, and if nothing that either of us does to reach or know God can fall outside the mercy and the providence of God, then we are indeed brothers and sisters. We are pilgrims, not strangers. We have much to learn from each other. We belong to God our common creator.[36]

Thus there are good grounds for extending the two-covenant theology now familiar in the context of Judaeo-Christian relations to allow for a multi-covenant theology derived from God's creation covenant with all peoples. No one will deny that in our relationship with the adherents of Judaism we seek to build on their existing relationship with God in order to communicate the claims of Christ upon their lives. We are also aware that our own awareness of those claims is deepened and clarified by our acquaintance with the history and beliefs of Judaism—hence our acceptance of the Old Testament into the Christian canon of Scripture. However, we are less willing to see a need for building on the 'Old Testaments' of other faith communities and their existing covenantal relationship with God as part of our evangelistic strategy. Neither are we keen to explore how their particular covenantal testimony enriches and illuminates the gospel we are so anxious to proclaim. Surely this is all because we have neglected God's universal covenant in our anxiety to affirm God's special and particular relationship with adherents of the Judaeo-Christian tradition—a particularity that is indeed scandalous in its proprietorial tendencies.

Yet we have much to gain evangelistically once we acknowledge that God is already in a convenantal relationship with those of other faiths—a covenant as inviolable as any made with the people of Israel. Of course, this does not mean that Hindus or Buddhists are 'right' in everything they believe and teach—no more than Judaism is deemed to be 'right' in all respects. What it does mean is that we should engage with those of other faiths on the assumption that God has been there before us, covenanting with them as their Creator and Lord. On this assumption, we not only find things in other faiths on which to develop our proclamation of the Christian covenant, but we also find our own relationship with God exposed to light from new and surprising sources.

It will be readily acknowledged that this approach to other faiths accords well with our principles of openness, honesty, variety and responsiveness. We remain open to the word of God expressed through various religious traditions, and respond appropriately with resources from our own tradition that, in its turn, is challenged and enriched by the encounter. As we would expect of an evangelistic strategy, good news is shared—*really* shared on all sides with a real turning to Christ taking place in the light of God's gracious turning to all who bear the image of their common Creator.

Seven ages—one faith?

Two trends in contemporary church life seem to be in apparent contradiction. On the one hand, we have seen the proliferation of groups aiming to attract those in specific age ranges—children, young people, young marrieds, young wives, Mothers' Union, men's fellowship, third-age groups, senior-citizens' clubs and so on. On the other, we are encouraged towards all-age worship and learning activities reflecting a model of the Church as 'family', with the emphasis on belonging and togetherness. This somewhat schizoid approach to local church life is indicative of our uncertainty as to whether growth in the Christian faith is related to a person's age or to their emotional, moral and cognitive development.

Many ministers have exploited this situation to advantage in the planning and delivery of so-called 'children's talks' in the context of family worship. Using the presence of children as the justification for making things as graphic and as simple as possible, the audio-visual aids are deployed with energy and imagination in order to get the message across. However, it is so often the adults who are all eyes and ears on such occasions, and many ministers have cheerfully accepted a back-handed compliment from adults who declare that they enjoyed and understood this morning's talk—with the clear implication that most conventional sermons sail serenely over their heads! This is simply because, in matters pertaining to faith, many an adult still 'thinks as a child' and is best nourished by milk rather than solid food (1 Corinthians 3.2). 'Faithing' is not necessarily age-specific, but societal assumptions that teaching must always be targeted on an age-related basis has inevitably influenced communication of the gospel in worship and through church-based organizations. The reality is that, although many things are still best managed in peer groupings, evangelism is not necessarily one of them. Ability to understand and respond to the claims of Christ on people's lives is likely to be more a matter of faith development than physical development, and that is the message of James Fowler and those who have taken up his research (entitled *Stages of Faith*).[37]

The temper and tone of this research has been summarized as follows:

> 'Faith' . . . as Fowler understands it, is essentially a way of knowing, valuing, being committed to, and understanding life. Faith gives meaning to our lives. It relates us to one another and to what we take to be ultimate, *our* discerned life-context. Faith is not specific to, or limited to, any one religion. It is not necessarily religious at all and may have a wide range of different contents that can be religious or semi-religious. . . . It is not, therefore, quite the same as what many Christians call 'The Faith' or 'Our Faith'. In the terms we are using here, those phrases refer to the content of Christian faith. Content is not our primary topic . . . it is faith-as-a-process, not faith-as-a-product, with which we are concerned. . . . Christian faith, according to Fowler, is 'the conversion and formation of human faith in and through relationship to God' which is mediated through Jesus, the Scriptures and teachings of the Church, and the Holy Spirit.[38]

For Fowler, faith has many aspects—including thinking, perspective-taking, moral judging, social awareness, relationship to authority, assimilation of symbols, and the formation of a world-view. The important point, though, is that the way of faith—the processes, structures and forms of faith—*develop* through various *stages* of faith. These stages can be numbered from 0 to 6 and can be labelled with almost impenetrable jargon (as is Fowler's wont) or simplified as 'Nursed Faith', 'Chaotic Faith', 'Ordering Faith', 'Confirming Faith', and so on.[39] The claim is that these stages are universal in that everyone might pass through them in principle, even if we don't get very far in practice. They are invariant (we cannot 'skip' a stage) and hierarchical (each stage follows on from the last).

Now there is no shortage of critics prepared to challenge Fowler on the grounds that he puts too little emphasis on the content of faith, or the possibility of conversion, or on the communal rather than individual dimension of faith. He is also attacked for the Western, liberal, middle-class and intellectual bias of his findings, and his research methods have also been subject to criticism. However, without being committed to every detail of his theory and methodology:

> . . . it is possible to view the work of Fowler and others as a useful tool with which to poke into the mechanics of faith. . . . While more careful empirical work is always needed, and theoretical criticism is absolutely essential, some of the central themes of faith development are too important . . . to be cavalierly ignored.[40]

Not least among these 'central themes' is the contention that people grow through stages of faith, but at a pace and to an extent not necessarily related to age or peer-group conventions. Stage 3 may be seen as a typically teenage stage, with its emerging ability to think abstractly and reflectively, although 'it is a time of going with a particular faith-current, or faith-crowd. There is no place for the individualistic "knight of faith" here, swimming against the tide.'[41] Yet who would deny that many adults are at this stage, and need a great deal of help and encouragement to move on to Stage 4, where people are prepared to choose and own a faith for themselves, whatever the pressures from their peer-group and social context? Likewise, if this arrival at a faith that is faith 'for me' is typical of the late teens or early twenties, there are many much older people who have never progressed to Stage 5, with its ability to live with less certainty and to be secure in an openness to other points of view. This 'balanced faith' demands a maturity often born out of pain and struggle, and few adults attain to it. This accounts for the headlong retreat into certainty that is such a troubling feature of faith-communities across the world as we approach the end of the millennium.

All this adds up to a necessity for evangelism to be alert and responsive to the stages of faith reached by those with whom we engage for the sake of the gospel. If mission audit is a tool of evangelistic research designed to enable an open, honest and plural response to the needs and perspectives of local communities, so faith development theory equips us to respond with equal flexibility and appropriateness to individuals—whatever stage they have reached in their journey towards meaning. This will, once again, involve listening before speaking. It will involve responding with imagination and sensitivity from the resources of our Christian tradition—a tradition that is more an account of believing than of beliefs, more about stages on a journey of discovery than about the contents of confessions and creeds.

Let there be no doubt that we are not denying content to the Christian gospel, or the need for that content to be rigorously examined and expounded in each generation. We are insisting, though, that the content of faith is at the service of faith development, and we contend that the gems of the gospel are rich in facets yet to be illuminated by interaction with those at various stages of faith. Paul found God in the Stage 1 'Chaotic Faith' of the Athenians and encouraged them to move on to a more 'Ordered (Stage 2) Faith', for which the 'unknown god' is now known and proclaimed. Thus we find God in that 'stage of faith' reached by our parishioner, or colleague, or neighbour and we help to develop their knowledge of God on the basis of what is already known. Having taken the trouble to ascertain and affirm the stage of faith our friend has reached, so we are all the better equipped to appreciate what it might mean to say Christ died for that person, and what face of Christ encounters that person most effectively. Bible and tradition are rich in resources placed at our disposal to help us answer these questions, and we must be prepared for things new as well as old to emerge from our treasury as we respond afresh in each new encounter.

Jesus in the Gospels encountered individuals as individuals and took account of their 'stage of faith' in the response he made to their particular question or situation. Indeed, much ink has been spilled in attempts to clarify just what Jesus meant by 'faith' on the various occasions when he declared 'your faith has saved you'. The faith of the woman with the issue of blood (Mark 5.25–34) seems to be at a very different level to that of the Canaanite woman with the demon-possessed daughter (Matthew 15.21–8) or the two blind men whose sight he restored (Matthew 9.27–31). 'Good news' for these people is essentially 'good news' for these *particular* people, and the face of Jesus they encountered and the salvation they experienced owes everything to his personal touch in response to a personal faith at a given stage in their growing into God.

Thus we may well wish to carry on providing seven different church-based organizations for the seven ages of human growth and development, but we must remember that when it comes to sharing and developing faith, ages are not equivalent to stages and the gospel cannot be automatically geared to age-specific groupings. This may mean that not only worship, but also other contexts for sharing the good news of God in Christ, need to be all-age (or rather, all-*stage*) experiences. This will not be an easy business, but we do have the appropriate means at our disposal. Stage 1 people are heavily into imagery and symbols, while Stage 2 folk will find meaning in stories—not least in biblical narratives and parables. Stage 3 people grow most effectively through a sense of belonging in fellowship with others, while Stage 4 people will want to turn symbols into concepts in order to check their own stance against other options on offer. Stage 5 people will have matured into what Paul Ricoeur calls a 'second naivety' where symbols, myths and rituals take on new power and significance.

When working with children, the symbols and stories appropriate to Stages 1 and 2 will be most in evidence, while the Stage 3 'need to belong' will be important when working with young people in their early teens. However, all five stages may be represented in adult groups, and skill will be needed to mix the necessary ingredients in such a way as to ensure that an effective response is made to the felt needs and aspirations of all present. This is not simply a case of orchestrating one tune to be heard on several instruments. Rather, we are creating an environment in which several tunes can be heard by those with ears attuned to hearing in very diverse ways. Thus we honour that flexibility and diversity that is characteristic of liberal evangelism and that is so essential if the 'Seven Ages of Man' are to be converted by the gospel of God into Seven Stages of Faith.

Non-spiritual non-direction?

Some years ago, a monk responded angrily (but with a twinkle in his eye) to a lecture I had given on spiritual direction. I don't think he was mad at me or even at the subject matter. It was the trendiness of it all that got to him. He said 'What I want is some non-spiritual non-direction!' He had a point. Spiritual direction can easily become too 'spiritual' in the sense of being ungrounded and unreal. It can become too directive by either being overly clinical or authoritarian. There is always the danger of the well-meaning or spiritually bossy charging into someone's life uninvited and doing some real damage. Some of us like to dabble in other people's lives and thus enlarge ourselves by interfering.[42]

This section is not meant to be in any sense yet another guide to the practice of spiritual direction—that would be way beyond the compass of this present volume. Alan Jones, though, has put his finger on an important element in spiritual direction, which puts it on all fours with a liberal approach to evangelism. Both evangelism and spiritual direction will benefit from being non-spiritual and non-directive in the sense indicated by the above quotation. Thus we move away from that triumphalist interventionism that has brought some attempts at evangelism and spiritual direction into disrepute, and affirm the need for some 'Holy Listening' and sensitive responding in the interests of openness, honesty and diversity.

In fact, Margaret Guenther's book is a powerful testimony to the effectiveness of listening, waiting and bringing to birth in the process of spiritual growth and development. Likewise, this is also an effective evangelistic process and, in so far as spiritual direction or pastoral counselling adheres to this model, to that extent it is the handmaid of evangelism. The spiritual director,

the non-directive counsellor and the liberal evangelist are all at
the work of bringing to birth what is already alive in the individual as made in the image of God. Each is a 'Midwife to the
Soul', enabling the seed now sown to grow into fruition. This
she does in a relationship of trust and mutual respect. Above all,
'she does things *with*, not *to*, the person giving birth'.[43]

Some spiritual direction is conducted with due formality and
in accordance with mutually agreed and understood procedures
—as when a young woman came to the priest's house and sat in
his study, while he drew from her slowly but surely the nature of
the burden now weighing so heavily on her conscience. At the
appropriate moment he invited her to accompany him to the church
for an act of formal confession and absolution weighted with the
gravitas that would be necessary for her acknowledgement of
true forgiveness. She rose from the *prie-dieu* a different woman,
going out into the world with dignity and full of thanksgiving for
the grace of God made known in her penitence. She was 'born-
again', and to that extent counselling, spiritual direction and
evangelism had coalesced into one work for the Kingdom.

On the other hand, spiritual direction can happen without the
least sign of sacramental formality—or even the use of the spoken
word! Indeed, I am committed to the 'theology of the grunt',
which can reach parts that mere words can never reach. I recall
one young man who came to my house a few months after his
wedding, at which I had officiated. He was very agitated. He and
his new wife had had their first row and she had stormed out of
the house leaving him in a state of extreme nervous tension. He
had walked the streets before finally knocking on my door. I
invited him in, showed him to a seat, and just let him talk—and
did he talk! All I did was simply grunt in a variety of tones,
sometimes encouraging, sometimes quizzical, sometimes non-
committal. After twenty minutes or so he wound down, looked
at his watch, and said, 'I had better go now—Joan will probably
be at home now, and I am sure it will be OK. Thank you, vicar,
for your good advice.' In fact, I had said nothing at all apart from
inviting him in—the rest had all been achieved by the God in
the grunt, calming and encouraging him so that a new self-
assurance and composure could be brought to birth sufficient to
send him on his way healed and hopeful. Again, counselling and
non-spiritual non-direction had elided into evangelism as good

news was brought to birth—this time through the midwifery of a flexibly responsive grunt!

Most clergy and lay people will recognize what is being described here. It is a matter of routine pastoral ministry and many will not feel the need to dignify it with any special name. This, though, is exactly what we are trying to say about evangelism. To some extent, the word needs demystifying so that a greater number of clergy and lay people can identify themselves with the Decade of Evangelism and be encouraged to build on their practice with greater awareness of the evangelistic dimension at the heart of it all. We are discovering in these sections that not only must a comprehensive evangelistic strategy include the tactics of flexible response, but any forms of Christian life and ministry that favour flexible response as an appropriate approach to pastoral care, worship, Bible study, spiritual direction, etc. have the right to be termed 'evangelistic' when we are taking the measure of mission in our localities. Experience seems to suggest that once people have been helped to see the evangelistic thrust of what they are already about, then they become less fearful of the word and more ready to explore a broad range of adventurous possibilities. If we allow the word to remain the exclusive property of hard-line evangelicals, then we automatically exclude from the Decade initiative those soft-centred servants of God whose very softness and centredness provide the essential resources for effective evangelism across the full range of Christian activity in the Church and in the community.

In that preface to Margaret Guenther's book with which we opened this section, Alan Jones continues:

> In some ways, the art of spiritual direction lies in our uncovering the obvious in our lives and in realising that everyday events are the means by which God tries to reach us. When Moliere's Bourgeois Gentilhomme discovered that all language was either poetry or prose, he was delighted to learn that he had been speaking prose all his life without knowing it. So with us. All along we've had a spiritual life and we didn't know it. There *is* poetry in the spiritual life but most of the time we are living in the prosaic mode.[44]

So it is with evangelism. It, too, has tended to be defined more and more narrowly and has become more and more mechanistic—

more a technique than a tendency. If everyday events are the means by which God tries to reach us, then it is through our everyday lives that God is very likely to reach other people. Of course, God will continue to reach them through major evangelistic events, though to a lesser extent than is sometimes assumed or claimed.[45] However, that is not the point. The point is that those who have been conditioned by much evangelical rhetoric into believing that they are evangelistically prosaic are in fact giving poetic witness to their faith in their open, honest and flexible responsiveness to those around them.

It is significant that when John Finney asked a survey sample to identify the main factors that influenced them in becoming Christian, their spouse/partner, Christian friends and the minister all left church activities, evangelistic events and Christian television/radio a long way behind.[46] In other words, it is under the influence of Christian lives that people are challenged to submit their own lives to the claims of Christ. Furthermore, this influence was exerted most effectively by those closest to them, who were able to respond to them best because they knew them best. Notice that it is the close and caring relationship that comes first, and the gospel finds its form and content in and through that relationship. Here we see Christian men and women drawing creatively on the resources of their own faith in order to respond effectively, and evangelistically, to those nearest to them. This is what we mean by liberal evangelism. There is a lot of it about, and if it is acknowledged and nurtured it will flourish in the future to even greater effect.

We observe that spirituality is fast becoming the common coinage of Christian communities across the broadest range of churchmanship and denominational allegiances. This has been well documented by Josephine Bax,[47] and the growing appetite for the great Christan classics and for the works of contemporary writers such as Kenneth Leech, Gerard Hughes and W. H. Vanstone testifies to the vitality of this trend. Gordon Jeff signified this break-out from the cloistered constraints that characterized much traditional spirituality with his *Spiritual Direction for Every Christian*,[48] and Weeks of Guided Prayer in the setting of daily life are growing alongside the burgeoning demand for a whole range of retreat and quiet-day experiences. People seem to want to supplement their local church diet from a varied menu ranging from Spring Harvest at Butlin's to month-long Ignatian retreats in remote religious houses. People are pretty eclectic in their tastes, so that all and sundry are prepared to have a try at all and sundry in order to slake their spiritual thirst! Of course, it is possible to see this as the trickle-down effect of the New Age movement, but that is to do less than justice to the extent and depth of this search for Christian spiritual experiences appropriate to the modern world yet in touch with tradition. It represents a distinct liberalizing of received spiritual conventions that were so often rooted in disciplined observance of a given rule and a specified way. Spirituality has become more marked by flexibility and responsiveness to individual and communal situations, and there is a refusal to accept that any one way holds the monopoly on spiritual wisdom. That is what liberal evangelism seeks to do for the vital task of sharing Christ in varied and appropriate ways. Gerard Hughes's *God of Surprises*[49] is not only at work in the realms of spirituality, showing us new things to treasure and new things to share as we open ourselves to divine creation and human creativity. This same God is at work in the spiritual intercourse between husband and wife, parent and child, friend and neighbour, so that evangelism breaks free from the skills-culture of evangelical 'Workshops' in order to be affirmed in the workplaces, living rooms and playgrounds where the face of Christ is focused in the faithfulness of a colleague or neighbour and good news of salvation is communicated through the open and honest graciousness of a friend.

It will be obvious by now that liberal evangelism revolves around certain basic principles that amount almost to a methodology. These principles were spelt out in chapter 3 and they have been applied to a number of week-by-week activities in local churches and communities. The number of sections could easily be extended to take account of additional issues and activities. Three of them merit some attention here:

Preparation

Much time (though probably not enough?) is now spent in preparation for baptism, marriage and initiation into adult membership. Model programmes are available in some profusion—I have a collection of some fifteen published confirmation courses and there is almost certainly plenty more where they came from. In recent years, good-quality printed publications and videos have been made available to assist in baptism and marriage preparation. Most denominations have special departments devoted to developing and promoting materials for good practice in these areas. Almost without exception, they acknowledge the opportunity provided by such ministries for teaching and sharing Christian faith, and an implicit evangelistic imperative is built into these courses. The tone and thrust of these evangelistic ingredients depends to a predictable extent on the sponsoring body or publishing house involved. In a few rare cases, that tone reflects something of the approach promoted here as liberal evangelism— in which case, they can usually be identified by the fact that they are now obviously out of date! That is, they have tried to respond appropriately to a prevailing culture, and subtle changes in social fashions and conventions quickly render outmoded a topical video or illustrated course-book. But at least the attempt has been made to observe and attend to the context of those participating in the programme, and this is a necessary starting point for effective evangelism. The next step is to enable these participants to express themselves with regard to their needs, values and aspirations—indeed, to articulate their stage of faith that triggers a response drawn from the resources of Bible and tradition, and appropriate to those confirmation candidates or those couples preparing for their wedding. As with the occasional offices, so with the preparation for them—the liberal approach to evangelism has a contribution to make.

Healing and deliverance

The same can be said for ministries of healing and deliverance. It is now accepted wisdom that the unqualified application of liturgical formulae or mechanical rituals in the context of such ministries leads to disastrous consequences in a large number of cases. The objectivization of evil, whether as disease or demon possession, tends towards a projection of reality out of and beyond the self that does not make for long-term wholeness and integrity. There is a prior need for the recipients of such ministries to be helped to take responsibility for themselves and what is happening to them, and manipulated exercises in psychological transference can be damaging in the extreme to those individuals subjected to them. There can be no doubt that the face of Jesus the healer or Jesus the exorcist might be the face of Christ most powerful to save in particular cases, but this can only be known after much listening and reflection. Ministries of healing and deliverance are essentially responsive ministries, and to the extent that they seek to respond with the face of Christ most appropriate to this person or set of circumstances, then to that extent they have their place in the repertoire of liberal evangelism. It may be the case that a post-Enlightenment world can and should have little place for what are often perceived by many liberals to be pre-Enlightenment palliatives. On the other hand, it is a thoroughly liberal position to argue that solutions are negotiated according to need rather than imposed according to prejudice. Who can deny that Jesus responded to the needs of his culture with a variety of solutions—including regular resort to ministries of healing and deliverance? The ways in which modern society now seeks to make sense of things tends to leave less room for such solutions to be commonly sought or received, but it amounts to an illiberal arrogance to write them out of the script when there remain those who have as legitimate a claim on the healing and exorcizing Christ as others have on Christ the teacher or liberator or friend.

Preaching

By no means least, all that we have said about liberal evangelism has implications for preaching. The oft-quoted definition of preaching as 'a monstrous monologue by morons to mutes' may do less than justice to most modern preaching, but there is a challenge to be faced here. A monologue, which is what the majority of sermons appear to be, sits ill with an evangelistic model that gives the priority to listening and responding. It is vital that monologue becomes dialogue, and the mutes are given a voice, or else preachers will deserve to be called moronic. This does not necessarily mean actual verbal exchanges as part of the ministry of the word (though it might), but it will mean that sermons are consciously prepared and delivered out of a listening mode. Most manuals on preaching today will emphasize that 'six

days shalt thou labour' in preparation for the Sunday sermon—
that is, the process begins on Monday morning with the reading
of the next Sunday's lections and the experiences and encounters
of the week become grist to the mill as the text takes shape as a
homily or sermon. Some of these encounters will arise from
pastoral ministry, although the preacher will be careful to protect
individuals' identities and their confidentiality. Much will be
gleaned from experiences shared through media coverage of
local and global events, so that the preacher fulfils Karl Barth's
requirement by entering the pulpit with the Bible in one hand
and the newspaper in the other.

This is not merely a matter of relevance or topicality. It is
basically about honouring our commitment to reality rather than
fantasy. It is driven by the conviction that the Christian message
is not a message in a bottle floated willy-nilly on the waters in
the hope that someone somewhere will receive it, but a word
made fresh in response to known needs and aspirations. 'Our
task,' wrote J. E. Powers, 'is to say the right things, to the right
people, in an acceptable way.' This sentiment is conveyed most
succinctly by James Cox's celebrated maxim: 'Preaching must
be as old as the truth it proclaims and as new as the day it is
done.' This accords well with our 'two-tunes' approach to faith
sharing.

When I was ordained in the early 1970s, I had only scant
respect for preaching as a viable means of communication in the
modern world. The merits of one-to-one relationships or small
group encounters were strongly promoted, as were the new
opportunities presented by the development of audio-visual
technology. We began to hear a great deal about concentration
spans and tolerance thresholds, so that the sermon of more than a
few minutes' duration was condemned as counter-productive.
Ministers in training were more likely to be referred to *Jackanory*
or *News at Ten* for examples of good practice than to the sermons
of Sangster or Spurgeon. It is difficult to include three points and
a conclusion in the average 'sound bite', so exegesis gave way to
story-telling, and exposition gave way to the six- or seven-minute
homily. As with the eighth-century prophets, so with the twentieth-
century preachers: they came with a word from the Lord, and all
the people wanted was a thought for the day!

However, it soon became clear to me that fairly traditional

preaching had more mileage left in it than the cynics seemed to suggest. While members of a typical congregation may be conditioned to receive electronic messages in small doses, they have considerably more stamina when it comes to the 'live' spoken word from the rostrum or the pulpit. However, the prevalence of the mass media had taught them to expect such communication to be direct, appropriate and responsive to their immediate situation. This premium on immediacy required the preacher to be existential as well as exegetical, so that preaching could indeed be 'as old as the truth it proclaims and as new as the day it is done'. Failure to respond consciously and sensitively to the immediacy of people's lives, rather than expounding the Scriptures so that people could respond positively and creatively in the light of their psychological and social situation, would soon find them voting with their feet. However, preaching that does take seriously the imperative to listen before speaking, to build on the 'old testaments' of those present and to respond with a face of Christ that meets them at their stage of faith and state of being, is still powerful in the cause of liberal evangelism. The challenge to respond is irresistible if the challenge is itself a response to the givenness of the situation, and the gift of the gospel will be accepted if indeed the right things are said, to the right people, in an acceptable way.

Yet we have not felt it necessary to give preaching the kind of profile that might be expected in a study of evangelism. This does not imply a devaluation of preaching, but it does reflect a fundamental fear that a mode of communication that so tempts us to talk *at* people rather than respond *to* them holds real dangers for a liberal approach to sharing the faith. There can be no doubt that preaching will continue to occupy a significant place in teaching and evangelistic ministries, but we do well to heed the principles of liberal evangelism as an effective antidote to persistent overemphasis on the pulpit as 'the parson's joy and his throne'. The role of the paternalistic pastor who knows what is best for his sheep and takes opportunities twice each Sunday to tell them so may have been appropriate in the social context of George Herbert's rural England, but it depended upon the message being known by the preacher and told to the hearer. This is to be commended as a valid and proven force in evangelical revivals across several centuries, but the pre-programmed pundit mouthing pious prescriptions uncontaminated by careless contact with prevailing culture can turn out to be too high a price to pay for a non-negotiated and non-negotiable gospel.

Yet preaching can consciously bend an ear to the needs and creeds of the modern world without thereby bowing the knee to the idols fashioned to articulate them. Indeed, it is only when the preacher bends an ear to the hearer that hearers will capture a word spoken in response to their yearnings and appropriate to their needs. Edouard Schweitzer said that it is 'the Preacher's job to take the words once spoken and make them speak again'. Perhaps so, but we would want to balance the requirement by urging that it is also the preacher's job to take words once *heard* and make them to be heard again. Words will not be heard if they are merely proclamations; they may be heard if they are experienced as sensitive responses drawn from the inexhaustible riches of an infinitely resourceful tradition. Speaking words that can be heard must be just as important as having ears with which to hear. Cultivating the communication of such words must be a priority for any preacher, and the principles of liberal evangelism have their place here as elsewhere.

Equipping the saints—a note on ministry and training[50]

In 1963 the ratio of full-time clergy to parishioners in the Church of England was 1 per 3,110 and the ratio to communicants was 1 per 160. By 1988 the ratio of full-time clergy to parishioners had reached 1 per 4,500 and the ratio to communicants was at 1 per 140. The population as a whole had fewer clergy to serve them by the late 1980s, while churchgoers had more. This meant that it had become correspondingly easier to operate an associational church than to meet the demands of a communal church. This may help to explain why there has been a growth in 'gathered' churches in recent years, especially in urban areas.

Yet we must be careful to avoid drawing unwarranted conclusions from selective evidence. These figures relate only to full-time clergy and take no account of increases in non-stipendiary ministry and lay ministry. While most of those involved in these ministries are firmly rooted in the parochial system (even most of those originally ordained to ministry in secular employment), still we are conscious of a growing tendency to affirm ministerial presence in the Monday-to-Saturday world of home, work and leisure. The experiences of those ordained to such a role has been quite extensively documented,[51] but little has been heard of the Monday-to-Saturday ministry of lay people—apart from the publication of the General Synod Board of Education report *Called to be Adult Disciples*, published in 1988.[52] Most people, though, acknowledge that this is where the real work of evangelism is likely to take place most effectively, and liberal evangelism certainly depends on the willingness and ability of Kingdom-based Christians to hear and respond in terms appropriate to their immediate context.

Being on the spot was a crucial ingredient in traditional forms of full-time ministry—especially when people lived, worked and played in more or less the same locality. Now there are too few clergy to be 'on the spot' in every place—and anyway, the dislocation of people's lives has shown the parochial model to be less and less effective as a means of being where people are for most of the time. So 'the spot' where ministers are meant 'to be' is likely to be the workplace, shopping centre, golf course or the Job Centre, rather than the home base. This is not to argue against the parochial system—it remains the single most effective means of ensuring a Christian presence in every community.[53] However, it is to argue for a more conscious sense of presence in the less accessible sectors of our society, and that is going to entail the continued development of ordained and lay ministries where needs currently go unattended and the gospel is hardly heard.

A liberal approach to evangelism entails a more flexible approach to the selection, training and deployment of ministers. Readiness to be not only 'on the boundary', but to cross boundaries in order to feel the pulse of the prevailing culture, and to hear the fluctuating heartbeat of a sometimes sane and a sometimes sick society, is crucial if our good news is to be realistically responsive and strong to save.

The catacombs in Rome hold the remains of 'Dionysius, presbyter and physician' and excavation of the cemetery at Tyre in Lebanon has revealed the burials of 'Adelphios, tapestry-maker and sub-deacon'; 'Theodorus, deacon and carpenter'; 'Anthony, deacon and goldsmith'.[54] We may not know how effective these craftsmen were at their trades, but we may assume that their faith was earthed in the culture that gave them their living, and was responsive to the shared experiences of those with whom they had to do. Patrick Vaughan comments on Theodorus 'presbyter, silversmith, the friend of all' that he probably '[used] his workshop not merely as a place of trade, but also as a place providing good opportunity for pastoral contacts—for the ability to chat while working is one of the enduring characteristics of craftwork'.[55]

This ability 'to chat while working'—or idling, playing, shopping, cooking or driving—remains a crucial element in that interplay of hearing and responding that makes potential evangelists of us all, but especially of those of us who are selected and trained for a ministry at and beyond the frontiers of the Church. To be equipped for this task will not necessarily entail radically different programmes from those devised for more traditional forms of ministry, although we will have to give greater weight to the local context of ministry and to the candidate's life experience than has been necessarily so in the past. Of more value will be the application of the principles of liberal evangelism to the training and development of God's people wherever they may be sent to serve and witness. To this task, we now turn.

How can clergy and lay people be equipped for liberal evangelism?

In one sense, we hesitate to offer an answer. After all, we have been arguing that evangelism has all too often become a matter of applying learned techniques and this can lead to a kind of functional elitism with 'world-renowned' and 'leading' evangelists accorded star billing on the basis of performance and results. Just as 'stars' in other walks of life acquire a following and are flattered by imitation, so highly publicized evangelists are admired, and their methods adopted and deployed by lesser mortals in less glamorous locations. Thus evangelists are set apart and separate from the routines of day-to-day discipleship at the consequent cost of excluding from their ranks those who may not have acquired the techniques, but who still fulfil the task. 'Schools of Evangelism' clearly run the risk of creating and perpetuating an elite and we would be cautious about promoting them as serviceable to our strategy.

However, this is not to say that there is not a job to be done in helping Christians to 'own' the evangelism in which they are already engaged, and to develop an awareness of their evangelistic potential in a wide range of contexts and relationships. Already we see tremendous acceleration in the provisions of lay training opportunities for those engaged in leading worship, pastoral care and religious education. Indeed, somebody somewhere will be found putting on courses in each of the areas identified in the preceding sections. However, it is unlikely that the evangelistic dimension of these activities will be explicitly addressed. Pastoral care, worship, education and adult discipleship are very often compartmentalized, and this may be necessary in order to meet the needs of modern modular programmes. Thus attention to evangelistic implications in each of these areas could provide the golden thread linking otherwise disparate disciplines. Of course, because the flexible response strategy is good practice in each of these areas anyway, it is even more appropriate to recruit the theme of liberal evangelism as a unifying feature across a wide range of lay-training provision.

Much the same can be said for ministerial training. The cause of integration has dominated curriculum studies in theological education for some years now, and a range of models has been approved as appropriate for delivering the ordained ministry our Church requires. In some cases, the integrating factor is the regular round of worship and spiritual discipline. In others, it is the collegial and ecclesiastical institution that binds together the parts. Elsewhere, the drive towards self-discovery and self-awareness controls the agenda; or it is the mission imperative that determines the programme and how it is conveyed. In a variety of more or less conservative evangelical colleges and courses, it will be the call to evangelism that provides the controlling principle. However, the kind of approach to evangelism that we are advocating has the potential to be used as syllabus cement across the whole spectrum of ministerial formation.

First of all, liberal evangelism embraces and affirms training in the human sciences that has become an established part of ministry training over the past twenty-five years. Professional ministers are in need of all the help they can get if they are going to be able to analyse and interpret the social and psychological data that is now available to them. This in turn will ensure that they are able to understand and appreciate with some degree of accuracy the complexities of the social situation in which they are set. If evangelism is about responding, then we must try to ensure that our ministers are responding to reality rather than fantasy, to things as they are rather than to things as they would wish them to be.

Secondly, though, the response is not to be that of the trained psychiatrist or social worker. Instead, the response is to be recognizably resourced by the tradition in which the minister stands as a representative interpreter. Contrary to the popular misconception, the liberal evangelist needs to be steeped in the tradition even more than his or her conservative colleague. This is because a premium is being placed on using the Bible and tradition creatively as tools, rather than dogmatically as given and non-negotiable sources. We have all encountered that kind of Christian who has learned a certain patter off by heart and simply repeats it whatever the situation. This can be relatively undemanding in terms of what it is necessary to know in order to get the message across, but, if we are in the business of resourcing our responses with faces of Christ and models of salvation mined from the hugely rich seams of Scripture and tradition, then the need for thorough and thoroughgoing training in biblical, doctrinal and historical studies is beyond question. Furthermore, such studies should encourage the full deployment of critical faculties in order to maximize the range of possible interpretations available for deployment in our evangelistic responses to the quest for meaning in contemporary cultures.

Finally, practical skills related to administration, planning, communication, pastoralia, liturgy, occasional offices and personnel management will also be grist to the evangelistic mill in so far as they ensure that appropriate frameworks are in place for the hearing and responding to be efficient and effective. Several times we have referred to creating an environment for this or that to happen, and this simply does not develop automatically. It depends on certain instincts and sensitivities that the minister is likely to possess more by grace than by education, but it also depends on acquired skills that must feature in any worthwhile course of ministerial formation.

Thus we see how liberal evangelism can provide a holding context for theological education. An agreed point of reference can do a great deal to ensure that curriculum development in ministerial training feels less like nailing jelly to a wall and more like nailing colours to the mast! And what more appropriate referent could there be in this Decade than liberal evangelism with all its potential to integrate the human sciences and historical theology in a common commitment to hearing and responding for the sake of the gospel. Helping people to listen before speaking, to use traditional resources creatively and to be open to new insights, will all be important in ministerial development. It may be, though, that liberal evangelism is more of an attitude of mind than a schedule of skills, and it is in the cultivation of appropriate attitudes that programmes of ministerial formation are ultimately to be judged. No amount of knowledge, and no amount of know-how, can compensate for misbegotten attitudes. The open, honest and flexibly responsive attitudes at the heart of liberal evangelism would seem to be central to the promotion of God's good news in this generation, and we could do no better than to use them as the standard against which to measure the content and delivery of theological education today.

Notes

1. W. A. Clebsch and C. Jaekle, *Pastoral Care in Historical Perspective.* Northvale, NJ, Aronson, 1975, p. 4.
2. Stephen Pattison, *A Critique of Pastoral Care.* Second edition, SCM Press 1993, pp. 11–12, 13.
3. Michael Jacobs, *Swift to Hear.* SPCK 1985.
4. Peter Speck, *Being There.* SPCK 1988.
5. Barbara and Tom Butler, *Just Mission.* Mowbray 1993, p. 13.
6. Norman Autton, *Touch: An Exploration.* Darton, Longman & Todd 1989.
7. Wesley Carr, *Brief Encounters: Pastoral Care through the Occasional Offices.* SPCK 1985.
8. Vance Packard, *The Hidden Persuaders.* New York 1957.
9. John Finney, *The Well-church Book.* Scripture Union and CPAS 1991.
10. Philip King, *Making Christ Known.* Church House Publishing 1992, p. 18.
11. John Finney, *Finding Faith Today.* Bible Society 1992, p. 110.
12. Dom Gregory Dix, *The Shape of the Liturgy.* Dacre Press–A & C Black 1964.
13. Paul Bradshaw, *The Search for the Origins of Christian Worship.* SPCK 1992.
14. For helpful reflections on this debate and its significance, see Michael Perham, ed., *The Renewed Book of Common Prayer.* Church House Publishing/SPCK 1993.

15. Archbishop's Commission on Urban Priority Areas, *Faith in the City*. Church House Publishing 1985, p. 135.
16. Ibid., p. 136.
17. Liturgical Commission, *Patterns for Worship*. Church House Publishing 1989.
18. Raymond E. Brown, *The Birth of the Messiah*. Geoffrey Chapman 1977, pp. 475–7.
19. Margaret Davies, in R. J. Coggins and J. L. Houlden, eds, *Dictionary of Biblical Interpretation*. SCM Press 1990, p. 578.
20. Frances Young, in Francis Watson, ed., *The Open Text*. SCM Press 1993, pp. 103–20.
21. Hans Reudi Weber, *Experiments with Bible Study*. Geneva, WCC, 1981.
22. See Anne Long, in J. Robson and D. Lonsdale, eds, *Can Spirituality be Taught?* ACATE 1983, pp. 115–20.
23. Walter Wink, *Transforming Bible Study*. Mowbray 1990.
24. Butler and Butler, *Just Mission*, pp. 8–9.
25. John Taylor, *The Christlike God*. SCM Press 1992, pp. 4–5.
26. See Alan Race, *Christians and Religious Pluralism*. SCM Press 1993.
27. David J. Bosch, *Transforming Mission*. New York, Orbis 1991, p. 483.
28. Keith Ward, *A Vision to Pursue*. SCM Press 1992.
29. Bosch, *Transforming Mission*, p. 483. See also M. Wiles, *Christian Theology and Inter-Religious Dialogue*. SCM Press 1992.
30. Contrary to Harold Netland's assumption that religious pluralism necessarily threatens evangelical claims to religious certainty (*Dissonant Voices*. Eerdmans 1991).
31. World Council of Churches Publications, *The Theology of the Churches and the Jewish People*. 1988, p. 111.
32. Anglican Consultative Council, *The Truth Shall Make You Free*. 1988, pp. 302–3.
33. For an illuminating treatment of this theme from the Jewish point of view, see Rabbi Tony Bayfield's article entitled 'Mission—A Jewish Perspective', *Theology*, May 1993, pp. 179–90.
34. Butler and Butler, *Just Mission*, p. 72.
35. World Council of Churches, *The Bible and People of Other Faiths*. 1987, pp. 2–3.
36. Ibid., pp. 10–11.
37. James Fowler, *Stages of Faith*. New York, Harper & Row 1981.
38. National Society/Church House Publishing, *How Faith Grows*. 1991, p. 8.
39. Ibid., pp. 19–35.
40. Ibid., p. 50.
41. Ibid., p. 25.
42. Alan Jones, in his Preface to Margaret Guenther's *Holy Listening: The Art of Spiritual Direction*. New York, Cowley, 1992, p. ix.
43. Ibid., p. 87.

44. Ibid., p. ix..
45. See Finney, *Finding Faith Today,* p. 68.
46. Ibid., p. 36.
47. Josephine Bax, *The Good Wine.* Church House Publishing 1986, and *Meeting God Today.* Church House Publishing 1990.
48. Gordon Jeff, *Spiritual Direction for Every Christian.* SPCK 1987.
49. Gerard Hughes, *God of Surprises.* Darton, Longman & Todd 1985.
50. Attention is drawn to the fact that this is only a 'Note'. There is considerable scope for the training implications of liberal evangelism to be explored at much greater length and depth than is possible here. However, this section may help to show how a good deal of ministerial training is already evangelistic in this liberal sense of the word, and could be even more so if this strategy is taken seriously.
51. See John Fuller and Patrick Vaughan, eds, *Working for the Kingdom.* SPCK 1986, p. 142; and Rod Hacking, *On the Boundary.* Canterbury Press 1990.
52. General Synod Board of Education, *Called to be Adult Disciples.* 1988.
53. See Giles Ecclestone, ed., *The Parish Church*; and Wesley Carr, ed., *Say One for Me.* SPCK 1992.
54. Fuller and Vaughan, *Working for the Kingdom*, p. 142.
55. Ibid.

5

In Conclusion . . .

In his magisterial study of historical and contemporary missiology, David Bosch identifies five 'missionary paradigms' that have dominated the understanding and development of Christian mission across the centuries and around the world.[1] He notes that the words 'evangelize' and 'evangelism' were revived and rehabilitated in church and mission circles during the nineteenth century after many centuries of disuse. It was with the slogan 'The evangelization of the world in this generation' that such terminology came truly into its own at the turn of this century. However, Bosch concludes that 'it remained difficult to determine precisely what authors mean by evangelism or evangelization', and he observes that David Barrett in his *Seven Hundred Plans to Evangelize the World* lists no less than seventy-nine definitions of evangelism 'to which many more could be added'.[2]

It will be noted that no precise definition of evangelism has been attempted in the preceding chapters. This is not simply because we have no wish to add to an already over-subscribed list of contenders. It is essentially because we do not see evangelism as a clearly defined activity of the Church alongside other activities, but as an attitude of mind and a way of being that permeates all that we do and are as Christians. Evangelism is an ever-present thread running through the mission of the Church, such that we would not wish to subscribe to Jurgen Moltmann's contention that 'Evangelization is mission, but mission is not merely evangelization.'[3] On such an analysis, the Church's serving, teaching, healing and liberating roles are seen as part of her mission, but separate from evangelism. This threatens to collude with John Stott's view that 'evangelism is one of two segments or components of mission, the other being social action'.[4] We would wish to affirm Bosch in his view that, 'Evangelism may never be given a life of its own, in isolation from the rest of the life and ministry of the Church.'[5] Hence our resistance to limited and limiting definitions.

However, we are conscious of the challenge that if evangelism is everything, and everything is evangelism, then is evangelism *really* anything at all? It may well be an attitude of mind, or a method, or an integrating thread, but does it have any content? This is the perennial challenge to liberalism in general, and it would not surprise us to hear it levelled against liberal evangelism in particular. The fact of the matter, though, is that the content of the gospel as promoted in this approach to evangelism simply could not be greater! It is not just the full gospel we are advancing, but a gospel full to overflowing. We have appealed constantly to the fecundity of the gospel that contains more than we need at any one time, and more than we yet know. Is it not so often the pedlars of non-negotiable certainties who limit the scope of the gospel so that the treasures taken from the store are always the old ones, whereas the householder in the parable can produce treasures old and new (Matthew 13.52)?

It is fascinating to note how many authors have developed the themes of diversity and variety in exploring what Bible and tradition have to say about God and Jesus and life in the Spirit. In addition to books by Pelikan, Schreiter and Wessels referred to in an earlier chapter, we also take account of John Bickersteth's *The Four Faces of God*[6] and Stephen Barton's *The Spirituality of the Gospels*.[7] There is a strong current of informed opinion ready to acknowledge a plurality of both content and presentation in the sources of Christian faith, and it is by the evangelistic celebration of such pluralism that sources become resources for sharing faith with appropriate flexibility in a myriad of personal and social situations. Far from being empty of content, our gospel is full to the brim with faces of Christ, models of salvation and spiritual surprises yet to be revealed as we enable the light of today to illuminate new facets of our multi-faceted inheritance.

While on the subject of likely challenges to this approach, we have to acknowledge that anything bearing the liberal label will tend to attract charges of collusion—and liberal evangelism will be no exception. As soon as it is suggested that the content of the message we share is governed to any significant extent by context, then tails will be deemed to be wagging dogs and carts will be presumed put before horses! However, we would want to maintain that in the cause of Christian evangelism we are called neither to collude nor collide with our prevailing sociological or psychological setting. In recent years, 'No Turning Back' has become synonymous with that kind of stubborn closed-mindedness that runs counter to the liberal spirit as defined in these pages. Yet so much evangelistic activity seems to set up a critical moment of collision between one set of beliefs and another, such that a choice has to be made to accept one set of claims and reject all others. No doubt there are sound New Testament texts in support of this scenario, but there seem to be equally sound New Testament texts in support of numerous evangelistic strategies—and we are as ill-advised to make unqualified and exclusive choices in this matter as in other matters relating to the life of the Spirit. As Philip King has pointed out, 'An "Anglican way of evangelism" will . . . be both pastoral and missionary and will recognise that for many people conversion is a process rather than a crisis.'[8] In other words, putting people on a collision course with contemporary culture may not necessarily be the most effective way to achieve evangelistic objectives, but neither will a policy of total collusion that simply baptizes any old beliefs in the interests of a rather patronizing inclusiveness. Some attitudes to other faiths seem to be collusive in this sense, as do some of the more sentimental interpretations of the role of the established Church in a pluralistic society. On Danbury Main Street, the two tunes neither colluded nor collided. Rather, they coincided in such a way as to allow Charles Ives to hear and embrace a musicality that challenged all his assumptions, but was yet attuned to his developing creativity. So it is with a liberal approach to evangelism. We have repeatedly emphasized the need for the tunes of tradition to be heard concurrently with the melodies of modernity, so that our approach to evangelism engineers neither a collusion nor a collision with the world-view or faith-claims of those with whom we engage as fellow pilgrims in our search for truth and as potential companions in our walk with Christ.

What we achieve is an open and honest encounter with communities and individuals that enables due account to be taken of the context in which they exist and due weight to be given to the gospel we seek to share. Overemphasis on the former can lead to collusion; overemphasis on the latter can lead to collision; a balancing of both can lead to conversion and, to that extent, liberals have their place alongside others in the economy of evangelism.

Conversion has always been the desired effect of evangelism, and it is the desired effect of liberal evangelism. However, it is not so much conversion from, or conversion to, but conversion as a state of being that characterizes the liberal approach. The struggle to achieve this can be illuminated by the struggle of the artist Georges Rouault 'to invest the commonplace with the aura of the miraculous [and] to create spiritual art in an age of faithlessness'.[9] He did not attempt to deny the reality of the world in which he lived, but neither could he deny the enduring power and validity of traditional forms of artistic expression:

> He invented his own iconography, but it was full of distant echoes, dim glimmerings of far older iconography. Painting Circus performers, acrobats whose bodies arc and stretch across dark voids while faceless multitudes look on, Rouault invented his own version of Golgotha. His clowns are metaphorical Men of Sorrows, contemporary Christs, images of loneliness and suffering and forbearance . . .
>
> 'You don't enter a tradition the way you get on a bus' said Rouault, 'It requires deeper and subtler affinities'. Rouault worked hard to establish the links between his own secular art and the religious art he wished to emulate: not just by evoking the old icons and stories of Christian legend, but by mimicking the effects of earlier devotional art.[10]

In the work of evangelism, the effect we are attempting to 'mimic' is the conversion effect of the gospel. However, we cannot achieve this by simply rerunning the traditional icons because, as Rouault recognized, the givenness of the situation is ever changing. Neither can we simply rubbish the old icons, because they proved effective and that effect needs affirming in each and every generation. So we invent our own iconography, but still 'full of distant echoes, dim glimmerings' of something far older. As the composer Aaron Copland put it: 'We are in search of a usable past.' As we respond to the world as it is, by fashioning icons drawn however obliquely from the icons of the world as it once was, so we participate in that conversion experience that enables us constantly to see a face of Christ in the world around us and the world around us in the face of Christ. 'You don't enter a tradition the way you get on a bus. It requires deeper and subtler affinities.' It is these 'deeper and subtler affinities' that liberal evangelism seeks to celebrate and share, so that the converting effects of the traditional icons can be renewed and rekindled in an iconography for today.

Thus we would want to argue that this approach to evangelism can be sustained against charges of guilt by association with liberalism. But how does it stand up to liberal anxieties about the ethos and ethics of evangelism? For example, evangelism has been seen as tantamount to proselytism, both at the inter-denominational and inter-faith levels. Are we not determined to persuade people out of one set of beliefs and into another? It is the often explicit triumphalism of such a project that excites the suspicion of liberals with regard to evangelism.

Yet we are careful here to see existing faith commitments not as rubble to be cleared from the site before building can begin, but as core foundation materials on the basis of which a Christian commitment can grow and develop. Commitment to the biblical concept of a creation covenant makes it possible for us to speak in terms of each person's 'old testament' as part of the givenness of the situation to which the liberal evangelist responds. This does not amount to adopting the other's faith into the Christian family—if this was so, then avoidance of proselytism would simply have led us into syncretism. However, it does encourage us to acknowledge with open and honest respectfulness the extent to which God has covenanted with a plurality of persons and communities, and has equipped us with a gospel resourceful enough to find a point of creative contact with the broadest spectrum of faiths and philosophies. Just as one orbiting space vehicle locks on to another and by virtue of the two-way com-munications between them a new space station is created, so Christianity seeks contact with other faiths and interlocks with them in such a way as to create yet another vehicle for Christ to be revealed and made known.

In their different ways, both proselytizers and syncretists want to change one set of beliefs into another. It is an essentially liberal contention that an open and responsive interrelationship between Christianity and other world-views and God-views can be mutually enriching, and the evangelistic dimension of such interrelationships should commend itself to liberal Christians, however suspicious they may have become of evangelism on other grounds.

Likewise, we can placate the sensitivities of those liberals who suspect evangelism for its excessive individualism and lack of a social conscience. Liberal evangelism has a necessary social dimension simply because of its emphasis on culture as a key component in the situation to which we make our response with the gospel. It has been argued that it is the Enlightenment itself that triggered the modern detachment of individuals from their social connections. However, the Enlightenment heralded a turn to the subject that does not necessarily entail a turning away from society. Indeed, a sense of community is at the heart of liberal democracy, with interdependence preferred to dependence or independence as the most appropriate model for corporate existence. The turn to the subject allows due worth to be allotted to the perceptions and insights of individual people, and the ideal society is one in which these diverse individual perspectives are pooled and shared in the interests of a more comprehensive and integrated vision. We have already argued that a church community that owns and celebrates the diversity of theological perceptions within its own number will be richer than one that enforces uniformity of belief and so excludes openness, honesty and diversity in the ranks. The same applies at the sociopolitical level, so that the subjectivity of the individual that sets each one apart from their neighbour is balanced by that sociality that requires us to be a part of our neighbourhood. Bosch affirms 'people are never isolated individuals. They are social beings, who can never be severed from the network of relationships in which they exist. And the individual's conversion touches all these relationships'[11] —and we would add: and all these relationships touch and shape the individual's conversion.

Liberal evangelism can never be merely about the conversion of individuals. The premium it places on culture and context will always find it attending to the cries and crises of society in order to bring into focus that face of Christ, that message of salvation that will challenge and change not only individual souls, but whole societies. Evangelism can never be limited to satisfying some people's spiritual needs, while most people's cries for justice, freedom and basic human dignity go unattended. Bosch captures our mood exactly:

Evangelism . . . means enlisting people for the reign of God, liberating them from themselves, their sins and their entanglements, so that they will be free for God and neighbour. It calls individuals to a life of openness, vulnerability, wholeness and love. To win people to Jesus is to win their allegiance to God's priorities. God wills not only that we be rescued from hell and redeemed for heaven, but also that within us—and through our ministry also in society around us—the 'Fullness of Christ' be re-created, the image of God be restored in our lives and relationships.[12]

If this is what evangelism is about, then liberals need have no suspicions on account of any failure in social responsibility. Indeed, we would argue that it is precisely the liberal approach that takes the givenness of the psycho-social situation as the starting point for evangelism, and the transformation of that situation as essential to its goal.

One of the main aims of this study has been to bridge the gap between liberalism and evangelism. The mutual suspicion that has characterized the relationship between these two major elements in the most recent Christian centuries has been detrimental to them both—and so to the well-being of the Church's mission in the modern world. We have sought to show that liberalism must have an evangelistic thrust to it if it is to lay claim to any Christian credibility; and we have argued that the openness, honesty and respect for diversity that are the marks of the liberal spirit are also the mark of a flexibly responsive evangelism. We have sought to demonstrate that evangelistic strategies that fail to make room for a liberal approach to evangelism will be missing out on a vital contribution to the sharing of good news both down our street and across our world. Liberals need to make room for evangelism, and evangelists need to find space for liberalism if this Decade is to be a sharing of faith on several fronts rather than a trading of insults across partition fences.

Above all, though, we have wanted to show that evangelism is already part of the normal life and witness of local churches and their members. Thus we confirm the conclusion of the deanery synod member who said after a presentation on the Decade: 'What you are really saying is that we need to do the same things, but better than before.'[13] In the course of our everyday lives we are engaging with people in a wide range of contexts, listening to them and responding as appropriately as we are able. Equally, through worship, Bible study and one-to-one contact with our fellow-Christians, we are assimilating our inheritance of salvation-history and spiritual wisdom. To bring together the day-to-day engagement of Christian people with their neighbours and the day-to-day engagement of Christian people with the sources and resources of their faith is to take an important step in the direction of affirming a day-to-day evangelism seldom dignified with the name, but worthy of it none the less. Should evangelism be included in the Christian's job description? We want to argue that evangelism *is* the Christian's job description, and experience suggests that many are fulfilling the task by their innate ability to respond to those around them appropriately and effectively with the good news of God in the person of Christ.

In his introduction to a recent book on Christian apologetics, Alister McGrath writes as follows:

> Responsible apologetics is based upon a knowledge both of the gospel and its audience. People have different reasons for not being Christians. They offer different points of contact for the gospel. An apologetics which is insensitive to human individuality and the variety of situations in which people find themselves is going to get nowhere—fast.
>
> Apologetics is a resource; it is up to the apologist to make the connections with the lives of real people in the modern world. Without this connection, theories remain theories, abstract ideas hanging in mid-air, and not grounded in the realities of life. But the history of Christian apologetics demonstrates that these connections *can* be made, just as the history of the church shows that they *must* be made. When all is said and done, apologetics is not about winning arguments—it is about winning people.
>
> The effective apologist is one who listens before speaking, and who makes every effort to link the resources of the Christian apologetic tradition both to the needs of that person, and their ability to handle argumentation and imagery. The art

of effective apologetics is hard work, in that it simultaneously demands mastery of the Christian tradition, an ability to listen sympathetically, and a willingness to take the trouble to express ideas at such a level and in such a form that the audience can benefit from it. Hard work, perhaps—but the results justify this investment of intellectual rigour and pastoral concern.[14]

Here is a great deal that we would want to affirm as characteristic marks of evangelism as we have been promoting it in these pages. We simply could not have put it better ourselves! Yet our commendation is tempered by the realization, subsequently confirmed by the rest of McGrath's book, that this flexibly responsive methodology is purely about presentation. What is to be communicated is pretty inflexible with respect to truth, and other world-views are clearly lumped together as 'modern rivals to Christianity'.[15] So we want to adopt McGrath's approach to apologetics as described in the above quotation, and apply it to the principles of evangelism. Furthermore, though, we would require that these principles should allow for provisionality of content as well as presentation, and for other world-views to be potential allies with Christianity in the quest for meaning, and not implacable rivals. It is these additional requirements that decide the distinctiveness of liberal evangelism. Yet this positive affirmation of provisionality, and creative engagement with pluralism, is only made possible by a commitment to the treasures of the Christian tradition, not as sources to be defended, but as resources to be discovered, developed and deployed.

By no means least, we want to re-emphasize that liberal evangelism is but one approach among many. Making Christ known in our generation, and sharing good news of salvation in a fast-changing world, must demand more flair and imagination than can possibly be encompassed by one particular programme or manual of techniques. It is fascinating to 'decode' the Decade in order to identify the theological and ecclesiastical assumptions behind any particular definition or recommended strategy. The fact is that there are already many different approaches to evangelism at work in the world, and liberal evangelism is but one of the numerous attempts to unlock the riches of the gospel for the temporal and eternal well-being of our neighbours in Christ.

As Charles Ives put it: 'This may not be the only way to write music, but it's a nice way; and, who knows, it may be the only real nice way?'

Notes

1. David J. Bosch, *Transforming Mission*. New York, Orbis, 1991.
2. Ibid., p. 409. See C. Marsh, *Questioning Evangelism*, Grove Books 1993, pp. 24–5, where a definition of liberal evangelism is hazarded –but reluctantly!
3. Jurgen Moltmann, *The Church in the Power of the Spirit*. SCM Press, 1975, p. 10.
4. John Stott, *Christan Mission in the Modern World*, Falcon 1975, quoted in Bosch, *Transforming Mission*, p. 412.
5. Ibid., p. 412.
6. John Bickersteth, *The Four Faces of God*. Kingsway 1993.
7. Stephen Barton, *The Spirituality of the Gospels*. SPCK 1992.
8. Philip King, *Making Christ Known*. Church House Publishing 1992, p. 5.
9. Andrew Graham-Dixon in *The Independent Magazine*, 6 March 1993, p. 37.
10. Ibid.
11. Bosch, *Transforming Mission*, p. 417.
12. Ibid., p. 418.
13. King, *Making Christ Known*, p. 33.
14. Alister McGrath, *Bridgebuilding*. IVP 1992, p. 188.
15. Ibid.

Index